MznLnx

Missing Links Exam Preps

Exam Prep for

Global Shift: Reshaping The Global Economic Map In The 21st Century

Dicken, 4th Edition

The MznLnx Exam Prep is your link from the texbook and lecture to your exams.
The MznLnx Exam Preps are unauthorized and comprehensive reviews of your textbooks.

All material provided by MznLnx and Rico Publications (c) 2010
Textbook publishers and textbook authors do not particpate in or contribute to these reviews.

MznLnx

Rico Publications

Exam Prep for Global Shift: Reshaping The Global Economic Map In The 21st Century
4th Edition
Dicken

Publisher: Raymond Houge
Assistant Editor: Michael Rouger
Text and Cover Designer: Lisa Buckner
Marketing Manager: Sara Swagger
Project Manager, Editorial Production: Jerry Emerson
Art Director: Vernon Lowerui

Product Manager: Dave Mason
Editorial Assitant: Rachel Guzmanji
Pedagogy: Debra Long
Cover Image: Jim Reed/Getty Images
Text and Cover Printer: City Printing, Inc.
Compositor: Media Mix, Inc.

(c) 2010 Rico Publications
ALL RIGHTS RESERVED. No part of this work
covered by the copyright may be reproduced or
used in any form or by an means--graphic, electronic,
or mechanical, including photocopying, recording,
taping, Web distribution, information storage, and
retrieval systems, or in any other manner--without the
written permission of the publisher.

Printed in the United States
ISBN:

For more information about our products, contact us at:
Dave.Mason@RicoPublications.com

For permission to use material from this text or
product, submit a request online to:
Dave.Mason@RicoPublications.com

Contents

CHAPTER 1
A New Geo-Economy — 1

CHAPTER 2
The Changing Global Economic Map — 6

CHAPTER 3
Technology: The `Great Growling Engine of Change` — 12

CHAPTER 4
`The State is Dead ... Long Live the State` — 16

CHAPTER 5
Doing Things Differently: Variations in State Economic Policies — 28

CHAPTER 6
Transnational Corporations: The Primary Movers and Shapers of the Global Economy — 39

CHAPTER 7
`Webs of Enterprise`: The Geography of Transnational Production Networks — 47

CHAPTER 8
Dynamics of Conflict and Collaboration: Both Transnational Corporations — 52

CHAPTER 9
`Fabricating Fashion`: The Textiles and Garments Industries — 57

CHAPTER 10
`Wheels of Change`: The Automobile Industry — 63

CHAPTER 11
`Chips With Everything`: The Semiconductor Industry — 69

CHAPTER 12
`Making the World Go Round`: The Financial Services Industries — 74

CHAPTER 13
`Making the Connections, Selling the Goods`: The Distribution Industries — 82

CHAPTER 14
Winners and Losers: An Overview — 87

CHAPTER 15
Making a Living in Developed Countries: Where Will the Jobs Come From? — 90

CHAPTER 16
Making a Living in Developing Countries: Sustaining Growth, Enhancing Equity — 95

CHAPTER 17
Making the World a Better Place — 102

ANSWER KEY — 114

TO THE STUDENT

COMPREHENSIVE

The *MznLnx* Exam Prep series is designed to help you pass your exams. Editors at MznLnx review your textbooks and then prepare these practice exams to help you master the textbook material. Unlike study guides, workbooks, and practice tests provided by the texbook publisher and textbook authors, *MznLnx* gives you **all** of the material in each chapter in exam form, not just samples, so you can be sure to nail your exam.

MECHANICAL

The MznLnx Exam Prep series creates exams that will help you learn the subject matter as well as test you on your understanding. Each question is designed to help you master the concept. Just working through the exams, you gain an understanding of the subject--its a simple mechanical process that produces success.

INTEGRATED STUDY GUIDE AND REVIEW

MznLnx is not just a set of exams designed to test you, its also a comprehensive review of the subject content. Each exam question is also a review of the concept, making sure that you will get the answer correct without having to go to other sources of material. You learn as you go! Its the easiest way to pass an exam.

HUMOR

Studying can be tedious and dry. MznLnx's instructional design includes moderate humor within the exam questions on occassion, to break the tedium and revitalize the brain

Chapter 1. A New Geo-Economy

1. The _____ consists of a number of economic theories which describe the nature of the firm, company including its existence, its behaviour, and its relationship with the market.

In simplified terms, the _____ aims to answer these questions:

1. Existence - why do firms emerge, why are not all transactions in the economy mediated over the market?
2. Boundaries - why the boundary between firms and the market is located exactly there? Which transactions are performed internally and which are negotiated on the market?
3. Organization - why are firms structured in such specific way? What is the interplay of formal and informal relationships?

Despite looking simple, these questions are not answered by the established economic theory, which usually views firms as given, and treats them as black boxes without any internal structure.

The First World War period saw a change of emphasis in economic theory away from industry-level analysis which mainly included analysing markets to analysis at the level of the firm, as it became increasingly clear that perfect competition was no longer an adequate model of how firms behaved. Economic theory till then had focussed on trying to understand markets alone and there had been little study on understanding why firms or organisations exist.

    a. Khazzoom-Brookes postulate   b. Technology gap
    c. Policy Ineffectiveness Proposition   d. Theory of the firm

2. In microeconomics, _____ is quite simply the conversion of inputs into outputs. It is an economic process that uses resources to create a good or service that is suitable for exchange. This can include manufacturing, storing, shipping, and packaging.
    a. MET   b. Red Guards
    c. Solved   d. Production

3. The _____ movement is movement of movements which are critical of the globalization of capitalism. Participants base their criticisms on a number of related ideas. What is shared is that participants stand in opposition to the unregulated political power of large, multi-national corporations and to the powers exercised through trade agreements.
    a. Anti-consumerism   b. Asset price inflation
    c. Overcapitalisation   d. Anti-globalization

4. _____ is that which is owed; usually referencing assets owed, but the term can also cover moral obligations and other interactions not requiring money. In the case of assets, _____ is a means of using future purchasing power in the present before a summation has been earned. Some companies and corporations use _____ as a part of their overall corporate finance strategy.
    a. Debt   b. Collateral Management
    c. Hard money loan   d. Debenture

5. _____ in its literal sense is the process of transformation of local or regional phenomena into global ones. It can be described as a process by which the people of the world are unified into a single society and function together.

This process is a combination of economic, technological, sociocultural and political forces.

a. Globally Integrated Enterprise
b. Globalization
c. Global Cosmopolitanism
d. Helsinki Process on Globalisation and Democracy

6. In economics, an _____ is any good or commodity, transported from one country to another country in a legitimate fashion, typically for use in trade. _____ goods or services are provided to foreign consumers by domestic producers. _____ is an important part of international trade.
  a. AD-IA Model
  b. Export
  c. ACCRA Cost of Living Index
  d. ACEA agreement

7. _____ is the increase in the average temperature of the Earth's near-surface air and oceans since the mid-twentieth century and its projected continuation. Global surface temperature increased 0.74 ± 0.18 °C (1.33 ± 0.32 °F) during the last century. The Intergovernmental Panel on Climate Change (IPCC) concludes that anthropogenic greenhouse gases are responsible for most of the observed temperature increase since the middle of the twentieth century, and that natural phenomena such as solar variation and volcanoes probably had a small warming effect from pre-industrial times to 1950 and a small cooling effect afterward.
  a. Dividend unit
  b. Consumer goods
  c. Global warming
  d. Controlled Foreign Corporations

8. _____ has been viewed as a process of increasing involvement of enterprises in international markets, although there is no agreed definition of _____ or international entrepreneurship. There are several _____ theories which try to explain why there are international activities.

Adam Smith claimed that a country should specialise in, and export, commodities in which it had an absolute advantage.

  a. Internationalization
  b. Unified growth theory
  c. Uppsala model
  d. Economic problem

9. _____ is the shortage of common things such as food, clothing, shelter and safe drinking water, all of which determine the quality of life. It may also include the lack of access to opportunities such as education and employment which aid the escape from _____ and/or allow one to enjoy the respect of fellow citizens. According to Mollie Orshansky who developed the _____ measurements used by the U.S. government, 'to be poor is to be deprived of those goods and services and pleasures which others around us take for granted.' Ongoing debates over causes, effects and best ways to measure _____, directly influence the design and implementation of _____-reduction programs and are therefore relevant to the fields of public administration and international development.
  a. Liberal welfare reforms
  b. Poverty map
  c. Growth Elasticity of Poverty
  d. Poverty

10. _____s is the social science that studies the production, distribution, and consumption of goods and services. The term _____s comes from the Ancient Greek οἰκονομῖα from οἶκος (oikos, 'house') + νὍμος (nomos, 'custom' or 'law'), hence 'rules of the house(hold)'. Current _____ models developed out of the broader field of political economy in the late 19th century, owing to a desire to use an empirical approach more akin to the physical sciences.
  a. Energy economics
  b. Opportunity cost
  c. Inflation
  d. Economic

Chapter 1. A New Geo-Economy

11. A _____ is a geographical region that has economic laws that are more liberal than a country's typical economic laws. The category '_____' covers a broad range of more specific zone types, including Free Trade Zones (FTZ), Export Processing Zones (EPZ), Free Zones (FZ), Industrial Estates (IE), Free Ports, Urban Enterprise Zones and others. Usually the goal of a structure is to increase foreign investment.
   a. Special Economic Zone
   b. Linder hypothesis
   c. Customs union
   d. Transfer problem

12. _____ or specialization is the specialization of cooperative labour in specific, circumscribed tasks and roles, intended to increase the productivity of labour. Historically the growth of a more and more complex _____ is closely associated with the growth of total output and trade, the rise of capitalism, and of the complexity of industrialization processes. Later, the _____ reached the level of a scientifically-based management practice with the time and motion studies associated with Taylorism.
   a. Division of labour
   b. Work-life balance
   c. Day labor
   d. Demarcation dispute

13. In finance, the _____ is the system that allows the transfer of money between savers and borrowers.

Put another way: the _____ is a set of complex and closely interconnected financial institutions, markets, instruments, services, practices, and transactions.

   a. Hedonimetry
   b. Foreign investment
   c. Financial system
   d. Lean consumption

14. _____ is a defined term that an economy with an increased emphasis on informational activities and information industry.

The vagueness of the term has three major sources. First, not surprisingly, there is no agreed-upon definition regarding the threshold of when an economy is _____ and when it is not.

   a. Autarky
   b. Indicative planning
   c. Intention economy
   d. Information economy

15. The _____ in Davos, Switzerland (January, 2003) triggered anti-globalization protests across Switzerland. Access to the town of Davos was blocked by the police of Grisons, with reinforcements from other cantons, and even Austrian police, which was unprecedented. On Saturday January 25, the day scheduled for a protest march in Davos, only selected protesters were allowed to pass.
   a. 1921 recession
   b. 100-year flood
   c. 130-30 fund
   d. World Economic Forum

16. _____ relates to decisions that define expectations, grant power, or verify performance. It consists either of a separate process or of a specific part of management or leadership processes. Sometimes people set up a government to administer these processes and systems.
   a. 130-30 fund
   b. 100-year flood
   c. 1921 recession
   d. Governance

17. _____ is a forum for 21 Pacific Rim countries (styled 'member economies') to cooperate on regional trade and investment liberalisation and facilitation. APEC's objective is to enhance economic growth and prosperity in the region and to strengthen the Asia-Pacific community. Members account for approximately 40% of the world's population, approximately 54% of world GDP and about 44% of world trade.
   a. ACCRA Cost of Living Index
   b. AD-IA Model
   c. ACEA agreement
   d. Asia-Pacific Economic Cooperation

18. The _____ is an economic and political union of 27 member states, located primarily in Europe. It was established by the Treaty of Maastricht on 1 November 1993, upon the foundations of the pre-existing European Economic Community. With a population of almost 500 million, the _____ generates an estimated 30% share (US$18.4 trillion in 2008) of the nominal gross world product.
   a. European Court of Justice
   b. ACCRA Cost of Living Index
   c. ACEA agreement
   d. European Union

19. The _____ is a trilateral trade bloc in North America created by the governments of the United States, Canada, and Mexico. The agreement creating the trade bloc came into force on January 1, 1994. It superseded the Canada-United States Free Trade Agreement between the U.S. and Canada.
   a. Case-Shiller Home Price Indices
   b. North American Free Trade Agreement
   c. Federal Reserve Bank Notes
   d. Demand-side technologies

20. In economics and finance, _____ is the practice of taking advantage of a price differential between two or more markets: striking a combination of matching deals that capitalize upon the imbalance, the profit being the difference between the market prices. When used by academics, an _____ is a transaction that involves no negative cash flow at any probabilistic or temporal state and a positive cash flow in at least one state; in simple terms, a risk-free profit. A person who engages in _____ is called an arbitrageur--such as a bank or brokerage firm.
   a. Options Price Reporting Authority
   b. Electronic trading
   c. Alternext
   d. Arbitrage

21. _____ is the removal or simplification of government rules and regulations that constrain the operation of market forces. _____ does not mean elimination of laws against fraud, but eliminating or reducing government control of how business is done, thereby moving toward a more free market.

The stated rationale for '_____' is often that fewer and simpler regulations will lead to a raised level of competitiveness, therefore higher productivity, more efficiency and lower prices overall.

   a. Macroeconomic policy instruments
   b. Deregulation
   c. Secular basis
   d. Fundamental psychological law

22. In economics and business decision-making, _____ are costs that cannot be recovered once they have been incurred. _____ are sometimes contrasted with variable costs, which are the costs that will change due to the proposed course of action, and prospective costs which are costs that will be incurred if an action is taken.

In traditional microeconomic theory, only variable costs are relevant to a decision.

a. Post-purchase rationalization
c. Halo effect
b. Hyperbolic discounting
d. Sunk costs

23. _____ is the corporate management term for the act of reorganizing the legal, ownership, operational or better organized for its present needs. Alternate reasons for restructing include a change of ownership or ownership structure, demerger repositioning debt _____ and financial _____.

a. Market value
c. Forecast period
b. Securitization
d. Restructuring

Chapter 2. The Changing Global Economic Map

1. _____ was a global military conflict which involved a majority of the world's nations, including all of the great powers, organized into two opposing military alliances: the Allies and the Axis. The war involved the mobilization of over 100 million military personnel, making it the most widespread war in history. In a state of 'total war', the major participants placed their entire economic, industrial, and scientific capabilities at the service of the war effort, erasing the distinction between civilian and military resources.
   - a. 1921 recession
   - b. 100-year flood
   - c. World War II
   - d. 130-30 fund

2. _____ or specialization is the specialization of cooperative labour in specific, circumscribed tasks and roles, intended to increase the productivity of labour. Historically the growth of a more and more complex _____ is closely associated with the growth of total output and trade, the rise of capitalism, and of the complexity of industrialization processes. Later, the _____ reached the level of a scientifically-based management practice with the time and motion studies associated with Taylorism.
   - a. Day labor
   - b. Demarcation dispute
   - c. Work-life balance
   - d. Division of labour

3. In microeconomics, _____ is quite simply the conversion of inputs into outputs. It is an economic process that uses resources to create a good or service that is suitable for exchange. This can include manufacturing, storing, shipping, and packaging.
   - a. Red Guards
   - b. Solved
   - c. MET
   - d. Production

4. _____s is the social science that studies the production, distribution, and consumption of goods and services. The term _____s comes from the Ancient Greek oá¼°κονομῖα from oá¼¶κος (oikos, 'house') + vÏŒμος (nomos, 'custom' or 'law'), hence 'rules of the house(hold)'. Current _____ models developed out of the broader field of political economy in the late 19th century, owing to a desire to use an empirical approach more akin to the physical sciences.
   - a. Energy economics
   - b. Inflation
   - c. Opportunity cost
   - d. Economic

5. _____ is the increase in the amount of the goods and services produced by an economy over time. It is conventionally measured as the percent rate of increase in real gross domestic product, or real GDP. Growth is usually calculated in real terms, i.e. inflation-adjusted terms, in order to net out the effect of inflation on the price of the goods and services produced.
   - a. ACCRA Cost of Living Index
   - b. ACEA agreement
   - c. AD-IA Model
   - d. Economic growth

6. _____ is any long-term change in the patterns of average weather of a specific region or the Earth as a whole. _____ reflects abnormal variations to the Earth's climate and subsequent effects on other parts of the Earth, such as in the ice caps over durations ranging from decades to millions of years.

In recent usage, especially in the context of environmental policy, _____ usually refers to changes in modern climate

   - a. 100-year flood
   - b. 130-30 fund
   - c. 1921 recession
   - d. Climate Change

Chapter 2. The Changing Global Economic Map

7. The _____ is a protocol to the United Nations Framework Convention on Climate Change (UNFCCC or FCCC), an international environmental treaty produced at the United Nations Conference on treaty is intended to achieve 'stabilization of greenhouse gas concentrations in the atmosphere at a level that would prevent dangerous anthropogenic interference with the climate system.' The _____ establishes legally binding commitments for the reduction of four greenhouse gases (carbon dioxide, methane, nitrous oxide, sulphur hexafluoride), and two groups of gases (hydrofluorocarbons and perfluorocarbons) produced by 'Annex I' (industrialized) nations, as well as general commitments for all member countries. As of January 14 2009, 183 parties have ratified the protocol, which was initially adopted for use on 11 December 1997 in Kyoto, Japan and which entered into force on 16 February 2005. Under Kyoto, industrialized countries agreed to reduce their collective GHG emissions by 5.2% compared to the year 1990.
    a. Carbon offset
    b. Green New Deal
    c. Greenhouse gases
    d. Kyoto Protocol

8. The Organization of the Petroleum Exporting Countries is a cartel of twelve countries made up of Algeria, Angola, Ecuador, Iran, Iraq, Kuwait, Libya, Nigeria, Qatar, Saudi Arabia, the United Arab Emirates, and Venezuela. The cartel has maintained its headquarters in Vienna since 1965, and hosts regular meetings among the oil ministers of its Member Countries. Indonesia withdrew its membership in _____ in 2008 after it became a net importer of oil, but stated it would likely return if it became a net exporter in the world.
    a. OPEC
    b. ACCRA Cost of Living Index
    c. AD-IA Model
    d. ACEA agreement

9. _____ in economics and business is the result of an exchange and from that trade we assign a numerical monetary value to a good, service or asset. If Alice trades Bob 4 apples for an orange, the _____ of an orange is 4 apples. Inversely, the _____ of an apple is 1/4 oranges.
    a. Price war
    b. Price book
    c. Premium pricing
    d. Price

10. In finance, the _____s between two currencies specifies how much one currency is worth in terms of the other. It is the value of a foreign natione;s currency in terms of the home natione;s currency. For example an _____ of 102 Japanese yen to the United States dollar means that JPY 102 is worth the same as USD 1.
    a. Exchange rate
    b. ACEA agreement
    c. ACCRA Cost of Living Index
    d. Interbank market

11. The term _____ is applied broadly to a variety of situations in which some financial institutions or assets suddenly lose a large part of their value. In the 19th and early 20th centuries, many financial crises were associated with banking panics, and many recessions coincided with these panics. Other situations that are often called financial crises include stock market crashes and the bursting of other financial bubbles, currency crises, and sovereign defaults.
    a. Market failure
    b. Macroeconomics
    c. Co-operative economics
    d. Financial crisis

12. In economics, a _____ is a general slowdown in economic activity over a sustained period of time, or a business cycle contraction. During _____s, many macroeconomic indicators vary in a similar way. Production as measured by Gross Domestic Product (GDP), employment, investment spending, capacity utilization, household incomes and business profits all fall during _____s.
    a. Treasury View
    b. Recession
    c. Leading indicators
    d. Monetary economics

13. In economics, an _____ is any good or commodity, transported from one country to another country in a legitimate fashion, typically for use in trade. _____ goods or services are provided to foreign consumers by domestic producers. _____ is an important part of international trade.
   a. ACCRA Cost of Living Index
   b. ACEA agreement
   c. AD-IA Model
   d. Export

14. The _____ is the difference between the monetary value of exports and imports in an economy over a certain period of time. It is the relationship between a nation's imports and exports. A positive _____ is known as a trade surplus and consists of exporting more than is imported; a negative _____ is known as a trade deficit or, informally, a trade gap.
   a. Rational expectations
   b. Marginal propensity to import
   c. SIMIC
   d. Balance of trade

15. The balance of trade (or net exports, sometimes symbolized as NX) is the difference between the monetary value of exports and imports in an economy over a certain period of time. It is the relationship between a nation's imports and exports. A favorable balance of trade is known as a trade surplus and consists of exporting more than is imported; an unfavorable balance of trade is known as a _____ or, informally, a trade gap.
   a. Trade deficit
   b. Computational economic
   c. Complementary asset
   d. Demographics of India

16. _____ is a forum for 21 Pacific Rim countries (styled 'member economies') to cooperate on regional trade and investment liberalisation and facilitation. APEC's objective is to enhance economic growth and prosperity in the region and to strengthen the Asia-Pacific community. Members account for approximately 40% of the world's population, approximately 54% of world GDP and about 44% of world trade.
   a. ACCRA Cost of Living Index
   b. Asia-Pacific Economic Cooperation
   c. ACEA agreement
   d. AD-IA Model

17. In finance, _____ is investment originating from other countries.See Foreign direct investment.
   a. Foreign investment
   b. Preclusive purchasing
   c. Demand side economics
   d. Horizontal merger

18. _____ is a comparative concept of the ability and performance of a firm, sub-sector or country to sell and supply goods and/or services in a given market. Although widely used in economics and business management, the usefulness of the concept, particularly in the context of national _____, is vigorously disputed by economists, such as Paul Krugman .

The term may also be applied to markets, where it is used to refer to the extent to which the market structure may be regarded as perfectly competitive.

   a. Competitiveness
   b. Debt moratorium
   c. Quota share
   d. Countervailing duties

19. In economics, an _____ is any good (e.g. a commodity) or service brought into one country from another country in a legitimate fashion, typically for use in trade.It is a good that is brought in from another country for sale. _____ goods or services are provided to domestic consumers by foreign producers. An _____ in the receiving country is an export to the sending country.

Chapter 2. The Changing Global Economic Map

a. Import
b. Economic integration
c. Import quota
d. Incoterms

20. _____ in its classic form is defined as a company from one country making a physical investment into building a factory in another country. It is the establishment of an enterprise by a foreigner. Its definition can be extended to include investments made to acquire lasting interest in enterprises operating outside of the economy of the investor.

a. Non-governmental organization
b. Federal Deposit Insurance Corporation
c. Financial Stability Forum
d. Foreign direct investment

21. In economics and finance, _____ represents passive holdings of securities such as foreign stocks, bonds none of which entails active management or control of the securities' issuer by the investor; where such control exists, it is known as foreign direct investment. Generally, this means the investor holds less than 10% of the total shares or less than the amount needed to hold the majority vote.

Some examples of _____ are:

- purchase of shares in a foreign company.
- purchase of bonds issued by a foreign government.
- acquisition of assets in a foreign country.

Factors affecting international _____:

- tax rates on interest or dividends (investors will normally prefer countries where the tax rates are relatively low)
- interest rates (money tends to flow to countries with high interest rates)
- exchange rates (foreign investors may be attracted if the local currency is expected to strengthen)

_____ is part of the capital account on the balance of payments statistics.

a. Fund administration
b. Retirement Compensation Arrangements
c. CAN SLIM
d. Portfolio investment

22. The term '_____' refers to the concept of collecting information and attempting to spot a pattern in the information. In some fields of study, the term '_____' has more formally-defined meanings.

In project management _____ is a mathematical technique that uses historical results to predict future outcome.

a. Coefficient of determination
b. Trend analysis
c. Probit model
d. Quantile regression

23. _____ is a Regional Trade Agreement among Argentina, Brazil, Paraguay and Uruguay founded in 1991 by the Treaty of Asunci>ón, which was later amended and updated by the 1994 Treaty of Ouro Preto. Its purpose is to promote free trade and the fluid movement of goods, people, and currency.

_____ origins trace back to 1985 when Presidents Ra>úl Alfons>ín of Argentina and Jos>é Sarney of Brazil signed the Argentina-Brazil Integration and Economics Cooperation Program or PICE .

   a. Free trade area   b. MERCOSUR
   c. 130-30 fund   d. 100-year flood

24. The phrase _____ and acquisitions refers to the aspect of corporate strategy, corporate finance and management dealing with the buying, selling and combining of different companies that can aid, finance, or help a growing company in a given industry grow rapidly without having to create another business entity.

An acquisition, also known as a takeover or a buyout, is the buying of one company (the 'target') by another. An acquisition may be friendly or hostile.

   a. Differential accumulation   b. Political economy
   c. Mergers   d. Peace dividend

25. The _____ is an economic and political union of 27 member states, located primarily in Europe. It was established by the Treaty of Maastricht on 1 November 1993, upon the foundations of the pre-existing European Economic Community. With a population of almost 500 million, the _____ generates an estimated 30% share (US$18.4 trillion in 2008) of the nominal gross world product.

   a. ACCRA Cost of Living Index   b. ACEA agreement
   c. European Court of Justice   d. European Union

26. _____ is a type of trade policy that allows traders to act and transact without interference from government. Thus, the policy permits trading partners mutual gains from trade, with goods and services produced according to the theory of comparative advantage.

Under a _____ policy, prices are a reflection of true supply and demand, and are the sole determinant of resource allocation.

   a. 100-year flood   b. 1921 recession
   c. Free Trade   d. 130-30 fund

27. The _____ is a trilateral trade bloc in North America created by the governments of the United States, Canada, and Mexico. The agreement creating the trade bloc came into force on January 1, 1994. It superseded the Canada-United States Free Trade Agreement between the U.S. and Canada.

   a. Demand-side technologies   b. Federal Reserve Bank Notes
   c. Case-Shiller Home Price Indices   d. North American Free Trade Agreement

28. _____ ndustrialization in North America, is the process of social and economic change whereby a human group is transformed from a pre-industrial society into an industrial one. _____ t is a part of a wider modernisation process, where social change and economic development are closely related with technological innovation, particularly with the development of large-scale energy and metallurgy production. _____ t is the extensive organisation of an economy for the purpose of manufacturing.

a. AD-IA Model
b. ACEA agreement
c. ACCRA Cost of Living Index
d. Industrialization

Chapter 3. Technology: The `Great Growling Engine of Change`

1. _____s is the social science that studies the production, distribution, and consumption of goods and services. The term _____s comes from the Ancient Greek oá¼°κονομῖα from oá¼¶κος (oikos, 'house') + vĭŒµος (nomos, 'custom' or 'law'), hence 'rules of the house(hold)'. Current _____ models developed out of the broader field of political economy in the late 19th century, owing to a desire to use an empirical approach more akin to the physical sciences.
   a. Energy economics
   b. Opportunity cost
   c. Inflation
   d. Economic

2. _____ is a comparative concept of the ability and performance of a firm, sub-sector or country to sell and supply goods and/or services in a given market. Although widely used in economics and business management, the usefulness of the concept, particularly in the context of national _____, is vigorously disputed by economists, such as Paul Krugman .

   The term may also be applied to markets, where it is used to refer to the extent to which the market structure may be regarded as perfectly competitive.

   a. Countervailing duties
   b. Competitiveness
   c. Quota share
   d. Debt moratorium

3. In economics, an _____ is any good or commodity, transported from one country to another country in a legitimate fashion, typically for use in trade. _____ goods or services are provided to foreign consumers by domestic producers. _____ is an important part of international trade.
   a. AD-IA Model
   b. ACEA agreement
   c. ACCRA Cost of Living Index
   d. Export

4. _____ is a type of trade policy that allows traders to act and transact without interference from government. Thus, the policy permits trading partners mutual gains from trade, with goods and services produced according to the theory of comparative advantage.

   Under a _____ policy, prices are a reflection of true supply and demand, and are the sole determinant of resource allocation.

   a. 130-30 fund
   b. 1921 recession
   c. 100-year flood
   d. Free Trade

5. During the Industrial Revolution, _____ replaced water power and muscle power (which often came from horses) as the primary source of power in use in industry. Its first use was to pump water from mines. The early steam engines were not very efficient, but a modified version created by James Watt gave engines the power to become a driving force behind the Industrial Revolution.
   a. 130-30 fund
   b. 1921 recession
   c. 100-year flood
   d. Steam power

6. A municipality is an administrative entity composed of a clearly defined territory and its population and commonly denotes a city, town or a small grouping of them. A municipality is typically governed by a mayor and a city council or _____ council.

   The notion of municipality includes townships but is not restricted to them.

a. 130-30 fund
b. 1921 recession
c. 100-year flood
d. Municipal

7. The process of _____ involves the introduction of a good or service that is new or substantially improved. This includes, but is not limited to, improvements in functional characteristics, technical abilities, or ease of use.
   a. Dogs of the Dow
   b. Microcap stock
   c. Refusal to deal
   d. Product innovation

8. _____ Management is the succession of strategies used by management as a product goes through its _____. The conditions in which a product is sold changes over time and must be managed as it moves through its succession of stages.

The _____ goes through many phases, involves many professional disciplines, and requires many skills, tools and processes.

   a. Tax profit
   b. Procurement
   c. Corporate tax
   d. Product life cycle

9. Economic interventionism or _____ is an action in a Market economy taken by a government, beyond the basic regulation of fraud and enforcement of contracts, in an effort to affect its own economy. Economic intervention can be aimed at a variety of political or economic objectives, such as promoting economic growth, increasing employment, raising wages, raising or reducing prices, promoting equality, managing the money supply and interest rates, increasing profits, or addressing market failures. The intervention may to direct, or indirect as in the case of indicative planning.
   a. AD-IA Model
   b. ACEA agreement
   c. ACCRA Cost of Living Index
   d. Economic Planning

10. _____, in microeconomics, are the cost advantages that a business obtains due to expansion. They are factors that cause a producere;s average cost per unit to fall as scale is increased. _____ is a long run concept and refers to reductions in unit cost as the size of a facility, or scale, increases.
    a. Economies of scale
    b. Economic production quantity
    c. Isoquant
    d. Underinvestment employment relationship

11. _____ is the state of being which occurs when a person, object, or service is no longer wanted even though it may still be in good working order. _____ frequently occurs because a replacement has become available that is superior in one or more aspects. Videotapes making way for DVDs

Technical _____ may occur when a new product or technology supersedes the old, and it becomes preferred to utilize the new technology in place of the old.

   a. Obsolescence
   b. ACCRA Cost of Living Index
   c. AD-IA Model
   d. ACEA agreement

12. _____ is any long-term change in the patterns of average weather of a specific region or the Earth as a whole. _____ reflects abnormal variations to the Earth's climate and subsequent effects on other parts of the Earth, such as in the ice caps over durations ranging from decades to millions of years.

Chapter 3. Technology: The `Great Growling Engine of Change`

In recent usage, especially in the context of environmental policy, _____ usually refers to changes in modern climate

- a. 130-30 fund
- b. 100-year flood
- c. 1921 recession
- d. Climate Change

13. The _____ is a protocol to the United Nations Framework Convention on Climate Change (UNFCCC or FCCC), an international environmental treaty produced at the United Nations Conference on treaty is intended to achieve 'stabilization of greenhouse gas concentrations in the atmosphere at a level that would prevent dangerous anthropogenic interference with the climate system.' The _____ establishes legally binding commitments for the reduction of four greenhouse gases (carbon dioxide, methane, nitrous oxide, sulphur hexafluoride), and two groups of gases (hydrofluorocarbons and perfluorocarbons) produced by 'Annex I' (industrialized) nations, as well as general commitments for all member countries. As of January 14 2009, 183 parties have ratified the protocol, which was initially adopted for use on 11 December 1997 in Kyoto, Japan and which entered into force on 16 February 2005. Under Kyoto, industrialized countries agreed to reduce their collective GHG emissions by 5.2% compared to the year 1990.

- a. Greenhouse gases
- b. Kyoto Protocol
- c. Green New Deal
- d. Carbon offset

14. Economics:

- _____, the desire to own something and the ability to pay for it
- _____ curve, a graphic representation of a _____ schedule
- _____ deposit, the money in checking accounts
- _____ pull theory, the theory that inflation occurs when _____ for goods and services exceeds existing supplies
- _____ schedule, a table that lists the quantity of a good a person will buy it each different price
- _____ side economics, the school of economics at believes government spending and tax cuts open economy by raising _____

- a. Demand
- b. Production
- c. McKesson ' Robbins scandal
- d. Variability

15. _____ is the production of large amounts of standardized products, including and especially on assembly lines. The concepts of _____ are applied to various kinds of products, from fluids and particulates handled in bulk to discrete solid parts to assemblies of such parts

_____ of assemblies typically uses electric-motor-powered moving tracks or conveyor belts to move partially complete products to workers, who perform simple repetitive tasks.

- a. Mass production
- b. 1921 recession
- c. 130-30 fund
- d. 100-year flood

Chapter 3. Technology: The `Great Growling Engine of Change`

16. In microeconomics, _____ is quite simply the conversion of inputs into outputs. It is an economic process that uses resources to create a good or service that is suitable for exchange. This can include manufacturing, storing, shipping, and packaging.
    a. MET
    b. Solved
    c. Production
    d. Red Guards

17. _____ refers to various social theories about production and related socio-economic phenomena. It has varying but related meanings in different fields, as well as for Marxist and non-Marxist scholars. The T-Ford became a symbol of effective mass production.
    a. Fordism
    b. Marginal rate of transformation
    c. Piece work
    d. Productivity

18. _____ is the name given to the dominant system of economic production, consumption and associated socio-economic phenomena, in most industrialized countries since the late 20th century. It is contrasted with Fordism, the system formulated in Henry Ford's automotive factories, in which workers work on a production line, performing specialized tasks repetitively. Definitions of the nature and scope of _____ vary considerably and are a matter of debate among scholars.
    a. Production function
    b. Labor problem
    c. Product Pipeline
    d. Post-Fordism

19. A _____ is a geographical region that has economic laws that are more liberal than a country's typical economic laws. The category '_____' covers a broad range of more specific zone types, including Free Trade Zones (FTZ), Export Processing Zones (EPZ), Free Zones (FZ), Industrial Estates (IE), Free Ports, Urban Enterprise Zones and others. Usually the goal of a structure is to increase foreign investment.
    a. Customs union
    b. Linder hypothesis
    c. Transfer problem
    d. Special Economic Zone

20. _____ according to Onuoha (2007) is the practice of starting new organizations or revitalizing mature organizations, particularly new businesses generally in response to identified opportunities. _____ is often a difficult undertaking, as a vast majority of new businesses fail. Entrepreneurial activities are substantially different depending on the type of organization that is being started.
    a. Intrapreneurship
    b. ACCRA Cost of Living Index
    c. ACEA agreement
    d. Entrepreneurship

21. _____ s are a type of administrative division, in some countries managed by a local government. They vary greatly in size, spanning entire regions or counties, several municipalities, or subdivisions of municipalities.

In Austria, a _____ or Bezirk is an administrative division normally encompassing several municipalities, roughly equivalent to the Landkreis in Germany.

    a. 100-year flood
    b. 130-30 fund
    c. 1921 recession
    d. District

Chapter 4. `The State is Dead ... Long Live the State`

1. _____ is a type of trade policy that allows traders to act and transact without interference from government. Thus, the policy permits trading partners mutual gains from trade, with goods and services produced according to the theory of comparative advantage.

Under a _____ policy, prices are a reflection of true supply and demand, and are the sole determinant of resource allocation.

   a. 100-year flood
   b. 130-30 fund
   c. 1921 recession
   d. Free Trade

2. The _____ is a trilateral trade bloc in North America created by the governments of the United States, Canada, and Mexico. The agreement creating the trade bloc came into force on January 1, 1994. It superseded the Canada-United States Free Trade Agreement between the U.S. and Canada.
   a. Demand-side technologies
   b. Case-Shiller Home Price Indices
   c. Federal Reserve Bank Notes
   d. North American Free Trade Agreement

3. _____s is the social science that studies the production, distribution, and consumption of goods and services. The term _____s comes from the Ancient Greek οἰκονομία from οἶκος (oikos, 'house') + νόμος (nomos, 'custom' or 'law'), hence 'rules of the house(hold)'. Current _____ models developed out of the broader field of political economy in the late 19th century, owing to a desire to use an empirical approach more akin to the physical sciences.
   a. Energy economics
   b. Opportunity cost
   c. Inflation
   d. Economic

4. _____ is the process by which the activities of an organization, particularly those regarding decision-making, become concentrated within a particular location and/or group.

In political science, this refers to the concentration of a government's power - both geographically and politically, into a centralized government.

   a. Centralization
   b. Product innovation
   c. Teaser rate
   d. Microcap stock

5. In economics, an _____ is any good or commodity, transported from one country to another country in a legitimate fashion, typically for use in trade. _____ goods or services are provided to foreign consumers by domestic producers. _____ is an important part of international trade.
   a. ACCRA Cost of Living Index
   b. ACEA agreement
   c. AD-IA Model
   d. Export

6. A _____ is an entity formed between two or more parties to undertake economic activity together. The parties agree to create a new entity by both contributing equity, and they then share in the revenues, expenses, and control of the enterprise. The venture can be for one specific project only, or a continuing business relationship such as the Fuji Xerox _____.
   a. Property right
   b. Business valuation
   c. Nexus of contracts
   d. Joint venture

Chapter 4. `The State is Dead ... Long Live the State`   17

7. An _____ is a person who has possession of an enterprise and assumes significant accountability for the inherent risks and the outcome. It is an ambitious leader who combines land, labor, and capital to create and market new goods or services. The term is a loanword from French and was first defined by the Irish economist Richard Cantillon.

   a. Entrepreneur
   b. Expansionary policies
   c. ACEA agreement
   d. ACCRA Cost of Living Index

8. A _____ is a business that is privately owned and operated, with a small number of employees and relatively low volume of sales. The legal definition of 'small' often varies by country and industry, but is generally under 100 employees in the United States and under 50 employees in the European Union. In comparison, the definition of mid-sized business by the number of employees is generally under 500 in the U.S. and 250 for the European Union.

   a. Farmshoring
   b. Cabotage
   c. Procurement
   d. Small Business

9. _____ is an economic system in which wealth, and the means of producing wealth, are privately owned. Through _____, the land, labor, and capital are owned, operated, and traded for the purpose of generating profits, without force or fraud, by private individuals either singly or jointly, and investments, distribution, income, production, pricing and supply of goods, commodities and services are determined by voluntary private decision in a market economy. A distinguishing feature of _____ is that each person owns his or her own labor and therefore is allowed to sell the use of it to employers.

   a. Creative capitalism
   b. Socialism for the rich and capitalism for the poor
   c. Late capitalism
   d. Capitalism

10. _____ is a fee paid on borrowed assets. It is the price paid for the use of borrowed money , or, money earned by deposited funds . Assets that are sometimes lent with _____ include money, shares, consumer goods through hire purchase, major assets such as aircraft, and even entire factories in finance lease arrangements.

    a. Internal debt
    b. Interest
    c. Asset protection
    d. Insolvency

11. The term _____ refers to government debt, expenditures and revenues, or to finance (particularly financial revenue) in general.

    - _____ deficit is the budget deficit of federal or local government
    - _____ policy is the discretionary spending of governments. Contrasts with monetary policy.
    - _____ year and _____ quarter are reporting periods for firms and other agencies.

    a. Drawdown
    b. Bucket shop
    c. Fiscal
    d. Procter ' Gamble

12. The _____ consists of a number of economic theories which describe the nature of the firm, company including its existence, its behaviour, and its relationship with the market.

Chapter 4. `The State is Dead ... Long Live the State`

In simplified terms, the _____ aims to answer these questions:

1. Existence - why do firms emerge, why are not all transactions in the economy mediated over the market?
2. Boundaries - why the boundary between firms and the market is located exactly there? Which transactions are performed internally and which are negotiated on the market?
3. Organization - why are firms structured in such specific way? What is the interplay of formal and informal relationships?

Despite looking simple, these questions are not answered by the established economic theory, which usually views firms as given, and treats them as black boxes without any internal structure.

The First World War period saw a change of emphasis in economic theory away from industry-level analysis which mainly included analysing markets to analysis at the level of the firm, as it became increasingly clear that perfect competition was no longer an adequate model of how firms behaved. Economic theory till then had focussed on trying to understand markets alone and there had been little study on understanding why firms or organisations exist.

  a. Policy Ineffectiveness Proposition b. Technology gap
  c. Khazzoom-Brookes postulate d. Theory of the firm

13. The General Agreement on Tariffs and Trade was the outcome of the failure of negotiating governments to create the International Trade Organization (ITO.) _____ was formed in 1947 and lasted until 1994, when it was replaced by the World Trade Organization. The Bretton Woods Conference had introduced the idea for an organization to regulate trade as part of a larger plan for economic recovery after World War II.
  a. General Agreement on Tariffs and Trade b. General Agreement on Trade in Services
  c. Dutch-Scandinavian Economic Pact d. GATT

14. The _____ was the outcome of the failure of negotiating governments to create the International Trade Organization (ITO.) GATT was formed in 1947 and lasted until 1994, when it was replaced by the World Trade Organization. The Bretton Woods Conference had introduced the idea for an organization to regulate trade as part of a larger plan for economic recovery after World War II.
  a. General Agreement on Trade in Services b. GATT
  c. Dutch-Scandinavian Economic Pact d. General Agreement on Tariffs and Trade

15. A _____ is a duty imposed on goods when they are moved across a political boundary. They are usually associated with protectionism, the economic policy of restraining trade between nations. For political reasons, _____s are usually imposed on imported goods, although they may also be imposed on exported goods.
  a. Tariff b. 130-30 fund
  c. 100-year flood d. 1921 recession

16. The _____ is an important selective, mainly private, international organization designed by its founders to supervise and liberalize international trade. The organization officially commenced on 1 January 1995, under the Marrakesh Agreement, succeeding the 1947 General Agreement on Tariffs and Trade (GATT.)

The _____ deals with regulation of trade between participating countries; it provides a framework for negotiating and formalising trade agreements, and a dispute resolution process aimed at enforcing participants' adherence to _____ agreements which are signed by representatives of member governments and ratified by their parliaments.

a. 2009 G-20 London summit protests

c. Bio-energy village

b. World Trade Organization

d. Backus-Kehoe-Kydland consumption correlation puzzle

17. In economics, an _____ is any good (e.g. a commodity) or service brought into one country from another country in a legitimate fashion, typically for use in trade.It is a good that is brought in from another country for sale. _____ goods or services are provided to domestic consumers by foreign producers. An _____ in the receiving country is an export to the sending country.

a. Economic integration

c. Incoterms

b. Import quota

d. Import

18. _____ is an economic theory that holds that the prosperity of a nation is dependent upon its supply of capital, and that the global volume of international trade is 'unchangeable.' Economic assets or capital, are represented by bullion (gold, silver, and trade value) held by the state, which is best increased through a positive balance of trade with other nations (exports minus imports.) _____ suggests that the ruling government should advance these goals by playing a protectionist role in the economy; by encouraging exports and discouraging imports, notably through the use of tariffs and subsidies.

_____ was the dominant school of thought throughout the early modern period (from the 16th to the 18th century.)

a. Consumer theory

c. Nominal value

b. Mercantilism

d. General equilibrium theory

19. _____ is the economic policy of restraining trade between states, through methods such as tariffs on imported goods, restrictive quotas, and a variety of other restrictive government regulations designed to discourage imports, and prevent foreign take-over of local markets and companies. This policy is closely aligned with anti-globalization, and contrasts with free trade, where government barriers to trade are kept to a minimum. The term is mostly used in the context of economics, where _____ refers to policies or doctrines which 'protect' businesses and workers within a country by restricting or regulating trade with foreign nations.

a. Digital economy

c. Knowledge economy

b. Protectionism

d. Google economy

20. An _____ is a type of protectionist trade restriction that sets a physical limit on the quantity of a good that can be imported into a country in a given period of time. Quotas, like other trade restrictions, are used to benefit the producers of a good in a domestic economy at the expense of all consumers of the good in that economy.

Critics say quotas often lead to corruption (bribes to get a quota allocation), smuggling (circumventing a quota), and higher prices for consumers.

Chapter 4. `The State is Dead ... Long Live the State`

    a. Agreement on Agriculture
    b. International Monetary Systems
    c. Economic integration
    d. Import quota

21. A _____ is:

- Rewrite _____, in generative grammar and computer science
- Standardization, a formal and widely-accepted statement, fact, definition, or qualification
- Operation, a determinate _____ for performing a mathematical operation and obtaining a certain result (Mathematics, Logic)
    - Unary operation
    - Binary operation
- _____ of inference, a function from sets of formulae to formulae (Mathematics, Logic)
- _____ of thumb, principle with broad application that is not intended to be strictly accurate or reliable for every situation. Also often simply referred to as a _____
- Moral, an atomic element of a moral code for guiding choices in human behavior
- Heuristic, a quantized '_____' which shows a tendency or probability for successful function
- A regulation, as in sports
- A Production _____, as in computer science
- Procedural law, a _____ set governing the application of laws to cases
    - A law, which may informally be called a '_____'
    - A court ruling, a decision by a court
- In the U.S. Government, a regulation mandated by Congress, but written or expanded upon by the Executive Branch.
- Norm (sociology), an informal but widely accepted _____, concept, truth, definition, or qualification (social norms, legal norms, coding norms)
- Norm (philosophy), a kind of sentence or a reason to act, feel or believe
- 'Rulership' is the concept of governance by a government:
    - Military _____, governance by a military body
    - Monastic _____, a collection of precepts that guides the life of monks or nuns in a religious order where the superior holds the place of Christ
- Slide _____

- '_____,' a song by Ayumi Hamasaki
- '_____,' a song by rapper Nas
- '_____s,' an album by the band The Whitest Boy Alive
- _____s: Pyaar Ka Superhit Formula, a 2003 Bollywood film
- ruler, an instrument for measuring lengths
- _____, a component of an astrolabe, circumferator or similar instrument
- The _____s, a bestselling self-help book
- _____ Project (Run Up-to-date Linux Everywhere), a project that aims to use up-to-date Linux software on old PCs
- _____ engine, a software system that helps managing business _____s
- Ja _____, a hip hop artist
    - R.U.L.E., a 2005 greatest hits album by rapper Ja _____
- '_____s,' a KMFDM song

a. Technocracy
b. Procter ' Gamble
c. Demand
d. Rule

22. In finance, the _____s between two currencies specifies how much one currency is worth in terms of the other. It is the value of a foreign natione;s currency in terms of the home natione;s currency. For example an _____ of 102 Japanese yen to the United States dollar means that JPY 102 is worth the same as USD 1.
   a. ACEA agreement
   b. Interbank market
   c. ACCRA Cost of Living Index
   d. Exchange rate

23. In finance, _____ is investment originating from other countries. See Foreign direct investment.
   a. Demand side economics
   b. Preclusive purchasing
   c. Foreign investment
   d. Horizontal merger

24. An _____ is the price a borrower pays for the use of money they do not own, for instance a small company might borrow from a bank to kick start their business, and the return a lender receives for deferring the use of funds, by lending it to the borrower. _____s are normally expressed as a percentage rate over the period of one year.

_____s targets are also a vital tool of monetary policy and are used to control variables like investment, inflation, and unemployment.

   a. Arrow-Debreu model
   b. ACCRA Cost of Living Index
   c. Enterprise value
   d. Interest rate

25. _____ is an offer (often competitive) of setting a price one is willing to pay for something. A price offer is called a bid. The term may be used in context of auctions, stock exchange, card games, or real estate transactions.
   a. Bidding
   b. Bord halfpenny
   c. Central limit order book
   d. Normal good

26. _____ is the acquisition of goods and/or services at the best possible total cost of ownership, in the right quantity and quality, at the right time, in the right place and from the right source for the direct benefit or use of corporations or individuals, generally via a contract. Simple _____ may involve nothing more than repeat purchasing. Complex _____ could involve finding long term partners - or even 'co-destiny' suppliers that might fundamentally commit one organization to another.
   a. Procurement
   b. Pre-emerging markets
   c. Golden umbrella
   d. Sole proprietorship

27. _____ is any long-term change in the patterns of average weather of a specific region or the Earth as a whole. _____ reflects abnormal variations to the Earth's climate and subsequent effects on other parts of the Earth, such as in the ice caps over durations ranging from decades to millions of years.

In recent usage, especially in the context of environmental policy, _____ usually refers to changes in modern climate

   a. Climate Change
   b. 130-30 fund
   c. 1921 recession
   d. 100-year flood

Chapter 4. `The State is Dead ... Long Live the State`

28. The _____ is a protocol to the United Nations Framework Convention on Climate Change (UNFCCC or FCCC), an international environmental treaty produced at the United Nations Conference on treaty is intended to achieve 'stabilization of greenhouse gas concentrations in the atmosphere at a level that would prevent dangerous anthropogenic interference with the climate system.' The _____ establishes legally binding commitments for the reduction of four greenhouse gases (carbon dioxide, methane, nitrous oxide, sulphur hexafluoride), and two groups of gases (hydrofluorocarbons and perfluorocarbons) produced by 'Annex I' (industrialized) nations, as well as general commitments for all member countries. As of January 14 2009, 183 parties have ratified the protocol, which was initially adopted for use on 11 December 1997 in Kyoto, Japan and which entered into force on 16 February 2005. Under Kyoto, industrialized countries agreed to reduce their collective GHG emissions by 5.2% compared to the year 1990.
   a. Kyoto Protocol
   c. Carbon offset
   b. Greenhouse gases
   d. Green New Deal

29. To _____ is to impose a financial charge or other levy upon a taxpayer by a state or the functional equivalent of a state.

_____es are also imposed by many subnational entities. _____es consist of direct _____ or indirect _____, and may be paid in money or as its labour equivalent (often but not always unpaid.)

   a. 130-30 fund
   c. 1921 recession
   b. Tax
   d. 100-year flood

30. A _____ or labor union is an organization of workers who have banded together to achieve common goals in key areas and working conditions. The _____, through its leadership, bargains with the employer on behalf of union members (rank and file members) and negotiates labor contracts (Collective bargaining) with employers. This may include the negotiation of wages, work rules, complaint procedures, rules governing hiring, firing and promotion of workers, benefits, workplace safety and policies.
   a. Trade union
   c. Consumer goods
   b. Guaranteed investment contracts
   d. Case-Shiller Home Price Indices

31. _____ is the removal or simplification of government rules and regulations that constrain the operation of market forces. _____ does not mean elimination of laws against fraud, but eliminating or reducing government control of how business is done, thereby moving toward a more free market.

The stated rationale for '_____' is often that fewer and simpler regulations will lead to a raised level of competitiveness, therefore higher productivity, more efficiency and lower prices overall.

   a. Fundamental psychological law
   c. Secular basis
   b. Macroeconomic policy instruments
   d. Deregulation

32. _____ is the incidence or process of transferring ownership of a business, enterprise, agency or public service from the public sector (government) to the private sector (business.) In a broader sense, _____ refers to transfer of any government function to the private sector including governmental functions like revenue collection and law enforcement.

The term '_____' also has been used to describe two unrelated transactions.

a. Compound empowerment
b. Privatization
c. Performance reports
d. Ricardian equivalence

33. The phrase _____, according to the Organization for Economic Co-operation and Development, refers to 'creative work undertaken on a systematic basis in order to increase the stock of knowledge, including knowledge of man, culture and society, and the use of this stock of knowledge to devise new applications [sic]'

New product design and development is more than often a crucial factor in the survival of a company. In an industry that is fast changing, firms must continually revise their design and range of products. This is necessary due to continuous technology change and development as well as other competitors and the changing preference of customers.

a. 100-year flood
b. Research and development
c. 130-30 fund
d. 1921 recession

34. _____ to the arrival of new individuals into a habitat or population. It is a biological concept and is important in population ecology, differentiated from emigration and migration.

_____ is a modern phenomenon.

a. Immigration
b. AD-IA Model
c. ACCRA Cost of Living Index
d. ACEA agreement

35.

_____ is, in very basic words, a position a firm occupies against its competitors.

According to Michael Porter, the three methods for creating a sustainable _____ are through:

1. Cost leadership - Cost advantage occurs when a firm delivers the same services as its competitors but at a lower cost;

2. Differentiation - Differentiation advantage occurs when a firm delivers greater services for the same price of its competitors. They are collectively known as positional advantages because they denote the firm's position in its industry as a leader in either superior services or cost;

3. Focus (economics) - A focused approach requires the firm to concentrate on a narrow, exclusive competitive segment (market niche), hoping to achieve a local rather than industry wide _____. There are cost focus seekers, who aim to obtain a local cost advantage over competition and differentiation focuser, who are looking for a local difference.

a. Chaos theory in organizational development
b. National Diamond
c. Six Forces Model
d. Competitive advantage

36. Economics:

- _____, the desire to own something and the ability to pay for it
- _____ curve, a graphic representation of a _____ schedule
- _____ deposit, the money in checking accounts
- _____ pull theory, the theory that inflation occurs when _____ for goods and services exceeds existing supplies
- _____ schedule, a table that lists the quantity of a good a person will buy it each different price
- _____ side economics, the school of economics at believes government spending and tax cuts open economy by raising _____

a. Variability
b. Production
c. McKesson ' Robbins scandal
d. Demand

37. _____ is a forum for 21 Pacific Rim countries (styled 'member economies') to cooperate on regional trade and investment liberalisation and facilitation. APEC's objective is to enhance economic growth and prosperity in the region and to strengthen the Asia-Pacific community. Members account for approximately 40% of the world's population, approximately 54% of world GDP and about 44% of world trade.

a. AD-IA Model
b. ACCRA Cost of Living Index
c. Asia-Pacific Economic Cooperation
d. ACEA agreement

38. The _____ is an economic and political union of 27 member states, located primarily in Europe. It was established by the Treaty of Maastricht on 1 November 1993, upon the foundations of the pre-existing European Economic Community. With a population of almost 500 million, the _____ generates an estimated 30% share (US$18.4 trillion in 2008) of the nominal gross world product.

a. ACCRA Cost of Living Index
b. European Court of Justice
c. ACEA agreement
d. European Union

39. The _____, 1949-1991, was an economic organization of communist states and a kind of Eastern Bloc equivalent to--but more geographically inclusive than--the European Economic Community. The military equivalent to the Comecon was the Warsaw Pact, though Comecon's membership was significantly wider. The Comecon was the Eastern Bloc's reply to the formation of the OEEC.

a. 100-year flood
b. 130-30 fund
c. 1921 recession
d. Council for Mutual Economic Assistance

40. _____ is a designated group of countries that have agreed to eliminate tariffs, quotas and preferences on most (if not all) goods and services traded between them. It can be considered the second stage of economic integration. Countries choose this kind of economic integration form if their economical structures are complementary.

a. 130-30 fund
b. MERCOSUR
c. 100-year flood
d. Free Trade Area

41. A _____ is a free trade area with a common external tariff. The participant countries set up common external trade policy, but in some cases they use different import quotas. Common competition policy is also helpful to avoid competition deficiency.

| a. Common market | b. Customs union |
| c. Bilateral Investment Treaty | d. Grey market |

42. Economic interventionism or _____ is an action in a Market economy taken by a government, beyond the basic regulation of fraud and enforcement of contracts, in an effort to affect its own economy. Economic intervention can be aimed at a variety of political or economic objectives, such as promoting economic growth, increasing employment, raising wages, raising or reducing prices, promoting equality, managing the money supply and interest rates, increasing profits, or addressing market failures. The intervention may to direct, or indirect as in the case of indicative planning.

| a. AD-IA Model | b. Economic Planning |
| c. ACCRA Cost of Living Index | d. ACEA agreement |

43. A _____ is a customs union with common policies on product regulation, and freedom of movement of the factors of production (capital and labour) and of enterprise. The goal is that the movement of capital, labour, goods, and services between the members is as easy as within them. This is the fourth stage of economic integration.

| a. Grey market | b. Competitiveness |
| c. Mutual recognition agreement | d. Common market |

44. _____ is sometimes referred to as _____, actually it means Economic Monetary Union.

First ideas of an economic and monetary union in Europe were raised well before establishing the European Communities. For example, already in the League of Nations, Gustav Stresemann asked in 1929 for a European currency (Link) against the background of an increased economic division due to a number of new nation states in Europe after WWI.

| a. Euro Interbank Offered Rate | b. European Monetary Union |
| c. Exchange rate mechanism | d. European Monetary System |

45. _____ is a Regional Trade Agreement among Argentina, Brazil, Paraguay and Uruguay founded in 1991 by the Treaty of Asunci>ón, which was later amended and updated by the 1994 Treaty of Ouro Preto. Its purpose is to promote free trade and the fluid movement of goods, people, and currency.

_____ origins trace back to 1985 when Presidents Ra>úl Alfons>ín of Argentina and Jos>é Sarney of Brazil signed the Argentina-Brazil Integration and Economics Cooperation Program or PICE .

| a. 100-year flood | b. Free trade area |
| c. 130-30 fund | d. MERCOSUR |

46. An economic and _____ is a single market with a common currency. It is to be distinguished from a mere currency union , which does not involve a single market. This is the fifth stage of economic integration.

| a. Customs union | b. Free trade zone |
| c. Commercial invoice | d. Monetary Union |

47. The Caribbean Community (_____), is an organisation of 15 Caribbean nations and dependencies. _____'s main purposes are to promote economic integration and cooperation among its members, to ensure that the benefits of integration are equitably shared, and to coordinate foreign policy. Its major activities involve coordinating economic policies and development planning; devising and instituting special projects for the less-developed countries within its jurisdiction; operating as a regional single market for many of its members (_____ Single Market); and handling regional trade disputes.
   a. 130-30 fund
   b. 1921 recession
   c. 100-year flood
   d. CARICOM

48. The _____, is an organisation of 15 Caribbean nations and dependencies. CARICOM's main purposes are to promote economic integration and cooperation among its members, to ensure that the benefits of integration are equitably shared, and to coordinate foreign policy. Its major activities involve coordinating economic policies and development planning; devising and instituting special projects for the less-developed countries within its jurisdiction; operating as a regional single market for many of its members (Caricom Single Market); and handling regional trade disputes.
   a. Caribbean Community
   b. 100-year flood
   c. 1921 recession
   d. 130-30 fund

49. A _____, reserve bank, or monetary authority is the entity responsible for the monetary policy of a country or of a group of member states. It is a bank that can lend money to other banks in times of need. Its primary responsibility is to maintain the stability of the national currency and money supply, but more active duties include controlling subsidized-loan interest rates, and acting as a lender of last resort to the banking sector during times of financial crisis (private banks often being integral to the national financial system.)
   a. Central Bank
   b. 100-year flood
   c. 130-30 fund
   d. 1921 recession

50. The _____ is one of the world's most important central banks, responsible for monetary policy covering the 16 member States of the Eurozone. It was established by the European Union (EU) in 1998 with its headquarters in Frankfurt, Germany.

The predecessor to the _____ was the European Monetary Institute.

   a. AD-IA Model
   b. European Central Bank
   c. ACCRA Cost of Living Index
   d. ACEA agreement

51. _____ refer to services provided by the finance industry. The finance industry encompasses a broad range of organizations that deal with the management of money. Among these organizations are banks, credit card companies, insurance companies, consumer finance companies, stock brokerages, investment funds and some government sponsored enterprises.
   a. Virtual Bidding
   b. Delta neutral
   c. Minimum acceptable rate of return
   d. Financial services

52. _____ is the political interaction of transnational actors aimed at solving problems that affect more than one state or region when there is no power of enforcing compliance.

Chapter 4. `The State is Dead ... Long Live the State`

Traditionally, governance has been associated with 'governing,' or with political authority, institutions, and, ultimately, control. Governance in this particular sense denotes formal political institutions that aim to coordinate and control interdependent social relations and that have the ability to enforce decisions.

- a. Global governance
- b. Simultaneous policy
- c. Multilateralism
- d. 100-year flood

53. _____ relates to decisions that define expectations, grant power, or verify performance. It consists either of a separate process or of a specific part of management or leadership processes. Sometimes people set up a government to administer these processes and systems.

- a. 1921 recession
- b. 100-year flood
- c. 130-30 fund
- d. Governance

Chapter 5. Doing Things Differently: Variations in State Economic Policies

1. _____ Group is one of the largest corporate conglomerates (Keiretsu) in Japan and one of the largest publicly traded companies in the world. Surugacho (Suruga Street) (1856), from One Hundred Famous Views of Edo, by Hiroshige, depicting the Echigoya kimono and money exchange store with Mount Fuji in background. Currently, the _____ Main Building (ä¸‰äº•æœ¬é¤¨), which houses Sumitomo _____ Banking Corporation, _____ Fudosan, The Chuo _____ Trust and Banking Co.

   a. 1921 recession
   c. Mitsui
   b. 130-30 fund
   d. 100-year flood

2. _____ is the removal or simplification of government rules and regulations that constrain the operation of market forces. _____ does not mean elimination of laws against fraud, but eliminating or reducing government control of how business is done, thereby moving toward a more free market.

The stated rationale for '_____' is often that fewer and simpler regulations will lead to a raised level of competitiveness, therefore higher productivity, more efficiency and lower prices overall.

   a. Macroeconomic policy instruments
   c. Secular basis
   b. Fundamental psychological law
   d. Deregulation

3. _____ is a type of trade policy that allows traders to act and transact without interference from government. Thus, the policy permits trading partners mutual gains from trade, with goods and services produced according to the theory of comparative advantage.

Under a _____ policy, prices are a reflection of true supply and demand, and are the sole determinant of resource allocation.

   a. 1921 recession
   c. Free Trade
   b. 100-year flood
   d. 130-30 fund

4. _____ is the incidence or process of transferring ownership of a business, enterprise, agency or public service from the public sector (government) to the private sector (business.) In a broader sense, _____ refers to transfer of any government function to the private sector including governmental functions like revenue collection and law enforcement.

The term '_____' also has been used to describe two unrelated transactions.

   a. Compound empowerment
   c. Privatization
   b. Ricardian equivalence
   d. Performance reports

5. _____ is a forum for 21 Pacific Rim countries (styled 'member economies') to cooperate on regional trade and investment liberalisation and facilitation. APEC's objective is to enhance economic growth and prosperity in the region and to strengthen the Asia-Pacific community. Members account for approximately 40% of the world's population, approximately 54% of world GDP and about 44% of world trade.

   a. Asia-Pacific Economic Cooperation
   c. ACCRA Cost of Living Index
   b. ACEA agreement
   d. AD-IA Model

Chapter 5. Doing Things Differently: Variations in State Economic Policies

6. The _____ is an economic and political union of 27 member states, located primarily in Europe. It was established by the Treaty of Maastricht on 1 November 1993, upon the foundations of the pre-existing European Economic Community. With a population of almost 500 million, the _____ generates an estimated 30% share (US$18.4 trillion in 2008) of the nominal gross world product.
   a. ACEA agreement
   b. ACCRA Cost of Living Index
   c. European Court of Justice
   d. European Union

7. The _____ is a trilateral trade bloc in North America created by the governments of the United States, Canada, and Mexico. The agreement creating the trade bloc came into force on January 1, 1994. It superseded the Canada-United States Free Trade Agreement between the U.S. and Canada.
   a. North American Free Trade Agreement
   b. Case-Shiller Home Price Indices
   c. Federal Reserve Bank Notes
   d. Demand-side technologies

8. A _____ is a business that is privately owned and operated, with a small number of employees and relatively low volume of sales. The legal definition of 'small' often varies by country and industry, but is generally under 100 employees in the United States and under 50 employees in the European Union. In comparison, the definition of mid-sized business by the number of employees is generally under 500 in the U.S. and 250 for the European Union.
   a. Cabotage
   b. Small Business
   c. Farmshoring
   d. Procurement

9. The _____ of 1974 (actually enacted January 3, 1975 as Pub.L. 93-618, 88 Stat. 1978, 19 U.S.C. ch.12) was passed to help industry in the United States become more competitive or phase workers into other industries or occupations. It created fast track authority for the President to negotiate trade agreements that Congress can approve or disapprove but cannot amend or filibuster. The fast track authority created under the Act extended to 1994 and was restored in 2002 by the _____ of 2002.
   a. Trade Act
   b. 1921 recession
   c. 130-30 fund
   d. 100-year flood

10. _____ is an economic system in which wealth, and the means of producing wealth, are privately owned. Through _____, the land, labor, and capital are owned, operated, and traded for the purpose of generating profits, without force or fraud, by private individuals either singly or jointly, and investments, distribution, income, production, pricing and supply of goods, commodities and services are determined by voluntary private decision in a market economy. A distinguishing feature of _____ is that each person owns his or her own labor and therefore is allowed to sell the use of it to employers.
    a. Socialism for the rich and capitalism for the poor
    b. Creative capitalism
    c. Late capitalism
    d. Capitalism

11. _____s is the social science that studies the production, distribution, and consumption of goods and services. The term _____s comes from the Ancient Greek οἰκονομία from οἶκος (oikos, 'house') + νόμος (nomos, 'custom' or 'law'), hence 'rules of the house(hold)'. Current _____ models developed out of the broader field of political economy in the late 19th century, owing to a desire to use an empirical approach more akin to the physical sciences.
    a. Energy economics
    b. Economic
    c. Inflation
    d. Opportunity cost

12. _____ refers to the actions that governments take in the economic field. It covers the systems for setting interest rates and government deficit as well as the labour market, national ownership, and many other areas of government.

Chapter 5. Doing Things Differently: Variations in State Economic Policies

Such policies are often influenced by international institutions like the International Monetary Fund or World Bank as well as political beliefs and the consequent policies of parties.

a. ACEA agreement
b. ACCRA Cost of Living Index
c. AD-IA Model
d. Economic policy

13. _____ is a comparative concept of the ability and performance of a firm, sub-sector or country to sell and supply goods and/or services in a given market. Although widely used in economics and business management, the usefulness of the concept, particularly in the context of national _____, is vigorously disputed by economists, such as Paul Krugman .

The term may also be applied to markets, where it is used to refer to the extent to which the market structure may be regarded as perfectly competitive.

a. Countervailing duties
b. Competitiveness
c. Quota share
d. Debt moratorium

14. The General Agreement on Tariffs and Trade was the outcome of the failure of negotiating governments to create the International Trade Organization (ITO.) _____ was formed in 1947 and lasted until 1994, when it was replaced by the World Trade Organization. The Bretton Woods Conference had introduced the idea for an organization to regulate trade as part of a larger plan for economic recovery after World War II.

a. General Agreement on Trade in Services
b. Dutch-Scandinavian Economic Pact
c. General Agreement on Tariffs and Trade
d. GATT

15. The _____ was the outcome of the failure of negotiating governments to create the International Trade Organization (ITO.) GATT was formed in 1947 and lasted until 1994, when it was replaced by the World Trade Organization. The Bretton Woods Conference had introduced the idea for an organization to regulate trade as part of a larger plan for economic recovery after World War II.

a. GATT
b. General Agreement on Tariffs and Trade
c. General Agreement on Trade in Services
d. Dutch-Scandinavian Economic Pact

16. A _____ is a duty imposed on goods when they are moved across a political boundary. They are usually associated with protectionism, the economic policy of restraining trade between nations. For political reasons, _____s are usually imposed on imported goods, although they may also be imposed on exported goods.

a. 130-30 fund
b. 1921 recession
c. 100-year flood
d. Tariff

17. In economics, an _____ is any good (e.g. a commodity) or service brought into one country from another country in a legitimate fashion, typically for use in trade.It is a good that is brought in from another country for sale. _____ goods or services are provided to domestic consumers by foreign producers. An _____ in the receiving country is an export to the sending country.

a. Import
b. Import quota
c. Incoterms
d. Economic integration

Chapter 5. Doing Things Differently: Variations in State Economic Policies

18. A _____ is a geographical region that has economic laws that are more liberal than a country's typical economic laws. The category '_____' covers a broad range of more specific zone types, including Free Trade Zones (FTZ), Export Processing Zones (EPZ), Free Zones (FZ), Industrial Estates (IE), Free Ports, Urban Enterprise Zones and others. Usually the goal of a structure is to increase foreign investment.
   a. Linder hypothesis
   b. Transfer problem
   c. Customs union
   d. Special Economic Zone

19. _____ is the economic policy of restraining trade between states, through methods such as tariffs on imported goods, restrictive quotas, and a variety of other restrictive government regulations designed to discourage imports, and prevent foreign take-over of local markets and companies. This policy is closely aligned with anti-globalization, and contrasts with free trade, where government barriers to trade are kept to a minimum. The term is mostly used in the context of economics, where _____ refers to policies or doctrines which 'protect' businesses and workers within a country by restricting or regulating trade with foreign nations.
   a. Digital economy
   b. Google economy
   c. Protectionism
   d. Knowledge economy

20. _____ is any long-term change in the patterns of average weather of a specific region or the Earth as a whole. _____ reflects abnormal variations to the Earth's climate and subsequent effects on other parts of the Earth, such as in the ice caps over durations ranging from decades to millions of years.

    In recent usage, especially in the context of environmental policy, _____ usually refers to changes in modern climate

   a. 130-30 fund
   b. 1921 recession
   c. 100-year flood
   d. Climate Change

21. The _____ is a protocol to the United Nations Framework Convention on Climate Change (UNFCCC or FCCC), an international environmental treaty produced at the United Nations Conference on treaty is intended to achieve 'stabilization of greenhouse gas concentrations in the atmosphere at a level that would prevent dangerous anthropogenic interference with the climate system.' The _____ establishes legally binding commitments for the reduction of four greenhouse gases (carbon dioxide, methane, nitrous oxide, sulphur hexafluoride), and two groups of gases (hydrofluorocarbons and perfluorocarbons) produced by 'Annex I' (industrialized) nations, as well as general commitments for all member countries. As of January 14 2009, 183 parties have ratified the protocol, which was initially adopted for use on 11 December 1997 in Kyoto, Japan and which entered into force on 16 February 2005. Under Kyoto, industrialized countries agreed to reduce their collective GHG emissions by 5.2% compared to the year 1990.
   a. Carbon offset
   b. Green New Deal
   c. Kyoto Protocol
   d. Greenhouse gases

22. In economics, an _____ is any good or commodity, transported from one country to another country in a legitimate fashion, typically for use in trade. _____ goods or services are provided to foreign consumers by domestic producers. _____ is an important part of international trade.
   a. ACCRA Cost of Living Index
   b. Export
   c. ACEA agreement
   d. AD-IA Model

Chapter 5. Doing Things Differently: Variations in State Economic Policies

23. _____ is the body of laws, administrative rulings, and precedents which address the legal rights of, and restrictions on, working people and their organizations. As such, it mediates many aspects of the relationship between trade unions, employers and employees. In Canada, employment laws related to unionized workplaces are differentiated from those relating to particular individuals.
   a. Labour movement
   b. 100-year flood
   c. 130-30 fund
   d. Labour law

24. _____ is a term used by international political economy scholars to refer to the phenomenon of state-led macroeconomic planning in East Asia in the late twentieth century. In this model of capitalism (sometimes referred to as state development capitalism), the state has more independent political power, as well as more control over the economy. A development state is characterized by having strong state intervention, as well as extensive regulation and planning.
   a. Multilateralism
   b. 100-year flood
   c. Simultaneous policy
   d. Developmental state

25. _____ is exchange of capital, goods, and services across international borders or territories. In most countries, it represents a significant share of gross domestic product (GDP.) While _____ has been present throughout much of history, its economic, social, and political importance has been on the rise in recent centuries.
   a. Intra-industry trade
   b. Incoterms
   c. Import license
   d. International Trade

26. _____ is a Regional Trade Agreement among Argentina, Brazil, Paraguay and Uruguay founded in 1991 by the Treaty of Asunci>ón, which was later amended and updated by the 1994 Treaty of Ouro Preto. Its purpose is to promote free trade and the fluid movement of goods, people, and currency.

_____ origins trace back to 1985 when Presidents Ra>úl Alfons>ín of Argentina and Jos>é Sarney of Brazil signed the Argentina-Brazil Integration and Economics Cooperation Program or PICE.

   a. MERCOSUR
   b. 100-year flood
   c. 130-30 fund
   d. Free trade area

27. The _____ was one of the most powerful agencies in the Japanese government. At the height of its influence, it effectively ran much of Japanese industrial policy, funding research and directing investment. In 2001, its role was taken over by the newly created Ministry of Economy, Trade, and Industry (METI.)
   a. 1921 recession
   b. 130-30 fund
   c. Ministry of International Trade and Industry
   d. 100-year flood

28. In finance, _____ is investment originating from other countries. See Foreign direct investment.
   a. Demand side economics
   b. Preclusive purchasing
   c. Horizontal merger
   d. Foreign investment

29. _____ is an economic theory that holds that the prosperity of a nation is dependent upon its supply of capital, and that the global volume of international trade is 'unchangeable.' Economic assets or capital, are represented by bullion (gold, silver, and trade value) held by the state, which is best increased through a positive balance of trade with other nations (exports minus imports.) _____ suggests that the ruling government should advance these goals by playing a protectionist role in the economy; by encouraging exports and discouraging imports, notably through the use of tariffs and subsidies.

Chapter 5. Doing Things Differently: Variations in State Economic Policies 33

_____ was the dominant school of thought throughout the early modern period (from the 16th to the 18th century.)

a. Nominal value
c. Mercantilism
b. General equilibrium theory
d. Consumer theory

30. The phrase _____ and acquisitions refers to the aspect of corporate strategy, corporate finance and management dealing with the buying, selling and combining of different companies that can aid, finance, or help a growing company in a given industry grow rapidly without having to create another business entity.

An acquisition, also known as a takeover or a buyout, is the buying of one company (the 'target') by another. An acquisition may be friendly or hostile.

a. Peace dividend
c. Differential accumulation
b. Political economy
d. Mergers

31. The Plaza Accord or _____ was an agreement between the governments of France, West Germany, Japan, the United States and the United Kingdom, agreeing to depreciate the US dollar in relation to the Japanese yen and German Deutsche Mark by intervening in currency markets. The five governments signed the accord on September 22, 1985 at the Plaza Hotel in New York City.

The exchange rate value of the dollar versus the yen declined by 51% from 1985 to 1987.

a. Mellonomics
c. Plaza Agreement
b. 100-year flood
d. Louvre Accord

32. _____ or _____ Fukyo (high yen recession) is a state in which the yen is high, or valuable compared to other currencies. Since Japan is highly dependent on exports, this can cause a recession.

a. ACCRA Cost of Living Index
c. AD-IA Model
b. ACEA agreement
d. Endaka

33. In economics, a _____ is a general slowdown in economic activity over a sustained period of time, or a business cycle contraction. During _____s, many macroeconomic indicators vary in a similar way. Production as measured by Gross Domestic Product (GDP), employment, investment spending, capacity utilization, household incomes and business profits all fall during _____s.

a. Treasury View
c. Leading indicators
b. Recession
d. Monetary economics

34. _____ ndustrialization in North America, is the process of social and economic change whereby a human group is transformed from a pre-industrial society into an industrial one. _____ t is a part of a wider modernisation process, where social change and economic development are closely related with technological innovation, particularly with the development of large-scale energy and metallurgy production. _____ t is the extensive organisation of an economy for the purpose of manufacturing.

Chapter 5. Doing Things Differently: Variations in State Economic Policies

a. ACCRA Cost of Living Index
b. ACEA agreement
c. AD-IA Model
d. Industrialization

35. An _____ is a type of protectionist trade restriction that sets a physical limit on the quantity of a good that can be imported into a country in a given period of time. Quotas, like other trade restrictions, are used to benefit the producers of a good in a domestic economy at the expense of all consumers of the good in that economy.

Critics say quotas often lead to corruption (bribes to get a quota allocation), smuggling (circumventing a quota), and higher prices for consumers.

a. Agreement on Agriculture
b. Economic integration
c. International Monetary Systems
d. Import quota

36. _____ is a broad label that refers to any individuals or households that use goods and services generated within the economy. The concept of a _____ is used in different contexts, so that the usage and significance of the term may vary.

Typically when business people and economists talk of _____s they are talking about person as _____, an aggregated commodity item with little individuality other than that expressed in the buy/not-buy decision.

a. Consumer
b. 1921 recession
c. 100-year flood
d. 130-30 fund

37. _____ are final goods specifically intended for the mass market. For instance, _____ do not include investment assets, like precious antiques, even though these antiques are final goods.

Manufactured goods are goods that have been processed by way of machinery.

a. Bulgarian-American trade
b. Fiscal stimulus plans
c. G-20 Leaders Summit on Financial Markets and the World Economy
d. Consumer goods

38. _____ is a reduction in the value of a currency with respect to other monetary units. In common modern usage, it specifically implies an official lowering of the value of a country's currency within a fixed exchange rate system, by which the monetary authority formally sets a new fixed rate with respect to a foreign reference currency. In contrast, (currency) depreciation is used for the unofficial decrease in the exchange rate in a floating exchange rate system.

a. Reserve currency
b. Petrodollar recycling
c. Texas redbacks
d. Devaluation

39. An _____ company is one which produces goods mainly for exports, rather than for the domestic market. The term is commonly used to describe factories in developing countries producing goods for developed countries.

Such companies are heavily dependent on the exchange rate, usually wanting their domestic currency to be weak, as this allows them to sell their products cheaply abroad.

a. Independent goods
b. Inferior good
c. Information good
d. Export-oriented

40. _____ sometimes called export substitution industrialization (ESI) or export led industrialization (ELI) is a trade and economic policy aiming to speed-up the industrialization process of a country through exporting goods for which the nation has a comparative advantage. Export-led growth implies opening domestic markets to foreign competition in exchange for market access in other countries. Reduced tariff barriers, floating exchange rate (devaluation of national currency is often employed to facilitate exports), and government support for exporting sectors are all an example of policies adopted to promote EOI, and ultimately economic development.
   a. Aras Free Zone
   b. Agreement on Agriculture
   c. Export Yellow Pages
   d. Export-oriented industrialization

41. A _____ is an object whose consumption increases the utility of the consumer, for which the quantity demanded exceeds the quantity supplied at zero price. _____s are usually modeled as having diminishing marginal utility. The first individual purchase has high utility; the second has less.
   a. Good
   b. Composite good
   c. Merit good
   d. Pie method

42. Economic interventionism or _____ is an action in a Market economy taken by a government, beyond the basic regulation of fraud and enforcement of contracts, in an effort to affect its own economy. Economic intervention can be aimed at a variety of political or economic objectives, such as promoting economic growth, increasing employment, raising wages, raising or reducing prices, promoting equality, managing the money supply and interest rates, increasing profits, or addressing market failures. The intervention may to direct, or indirect as in the case of indicative planning.
   a. AD-IA Model
   b. ACCRA Cost of Living Index
   c. ACEA agreement
   d. Economic Planning

43. _____ is a system of economic, political, and social organization where social groups or interest groups, such as business, ethnic, farmer, labour, military are joined together under a common governing jurisdiction to try to achieve societal harmony and promote coordinated development. _____ is based on the sociological concept of functionalism.

The word '_____' is derived from the Latin word for body, corpus.

   a. Adolph Fischer
   b. Adam Smith
   c. Adolf Hitler
   d. Corporatism

44. _____s (also agrarian reform, though that can have a broader meaning) is an often-controversial alteration in the societal arrangements whereby government administers possession and use of land. _____ may consist of a government-initiated or government-backed real estate property redistribution, generally of agricultural land, or be part of an even more revolutionary program that may include forcible removal of an existing government that is seen to oppose such reforms.

Throughout history, popular discontent with land-related institutions has been one of the most common factors in provoking revolutionary movements and other social upheavals.

a. Putting-out system   b. Hanseatic League
c. Neomercantilism   d. Land reform

45. _____ is the process of sharing of skills, knowledge, technologies, methods of manufacturing, samples of manufacturing and facilities among governments and other institutions to ensure that scientific and technological developments are accessible to a wider range of users who can then further develop and exploit the technology into new products, processes, applications, materials or services. It is closely related to (and may arguably be considered a subset of) Knowledge transfer. Related terms, used almost synonymously, include 'technology valorisation' and 'technology commercialisation'.
a. Technology transfer   b. Judgment summons
c. Law of increasing relative cost   d. Patent

46. The term financial crisis is applied broadly to a variety of situations in which some financial institutions or assets suddenly lose a large part of their value. In the 19th and early 20th centuries, many _____ were associated with banking panics, and many recessions coincided with these panics. Other situations that are often called _____ include stock market crashes and the bursting of other financial bubbles, currency crises, and sovereign defaults.
a. General equilibrium   b. Microeconomics
c. Georgism   d. Financial crises

47. _____ is the development of economic wealth of countries or regions for the well-being of their inhabitants. It is the process by which a nation improves the economic, political, and social well being of its people. From a policy perspective, _____ can be defined as efforts that seek to improve the economic well-being and quality of life for a community by creating and/or retaining jobs and supporting or growing incomes and the tax base.
a. Economic Development   b. Experimental economics
c. Economic methodology   d. Inflation

48. A _____ or free zone (US: Foreign-Trade Zone) is a port or area with relaxed jurisdiction with respect to the country of location. Free economic zones may also be called _____s.

Most commonly a _____ is a special customs area with favorable customs regulations (or no customs duties and controls for transshipment.)

a. 130-30 fund   b. 100-year flood
c. Free port   d. Purchasing

49. _____ primarily refers to guidelines and interventions for the changing, maintenance or creation of living conditions that are conducive to human welfare. Thus, _____ is that part of public policy that has to do with social issues. The Malcolm Wiener Center for _____ at Harvard University describes it as 'public policy and practice in the areas of health care, human services, criminal justice, inequality, education, and labor' _____ is also distinct as an academic field.
a. 130-30 fund   b. 100-year flood
c. Social policy   d. 1921 recession

Chapter 5. Doing Things Differently: Variations in State Economic Policies

50. A _____ or labor union is an organization of workers who have banded together to achieve common goals in key areas and working conditions. The _____, through its leadership, bargains with the employer on behalf of union members (rank and file members) and negotiates labor contracts (Collective bargaining) with employers. This may include the negotiation of wages, work rules, complaint procedures, rules governing hiring, firing and promotion of workers, benefits, workplace safety and policies.

- a. Trade union
- b. Case-Shiller Home Price Indices
- c. Guaranteed investment contracts
- d. Consumer goods

51. The phrase _____, according to the Organization for Economic Co-operation and Development, refers to 'creative work undertaken on a systematic basis in order to increase the stock of knowledge, including knowledge of man, culture and society, and the use of this stock of knowledge to devise new applications [sic]'

New product design and development is more than often a crucial factor in the survival of a company. In an industry that is fast changing, firms must continually revise their design and range of products. This is necessary due to continuous technology change and development as well as other competitors and the changing preference of customers.

- a. 100-year flood
- b. Research and development
- c. 130-30 fund
- d. 1921 recession

52. A _____, state-owned enterprise or government business enterprise is a legal entity created by a government to undertake commercial or business activities on behalf of an owner government. There is no standard definition of a _____ or state-owned enterprise (SOE), although the two terms can be used inter-changeably. The defining characteristics are that they have a distinct legal form and they are established to operate in commercial affairs.

- a. Citizens for an Alternative Tax System
- b. Government-owned corporation
- c. Luxembourg Income Study
- d. Non-governmental organization

53. The _____ is an important selective, mainly private, international organization designed by its founders to supervise and liberalize international trade. The organization officially commenced on 1 January 1995, under the Marrakesh Agreement, succeeding the 1947 General Agreement on Tariffs and Trade (GATT.)

The _____ deals with regulation of trade between participating countries; it provides a framework for negotiating and formalising trade agreements, and a dispute resolution process aimed at enforcing participants' adherence to _____ agreements which are signed by representatives of member governments and ratified by their parliaments.

- a. Bio-energy village
- b. World Trade Organization
- c. Backus-Kehoe-Kydland consumption correlation puzzle
- d. 2009 G-20 London summit protests

54. _____ in economics and business is the result of an exchange and from that trade we assign a numerical monetary value to a good, service or asset. If Alice trades Bob 4 apples for an orange, the _____ of an orange is 4 apples. Inversely, the _____ of an apple is 1/4 oranges.

- a. Premium pricing
- b. Price
- c. Price war
- d. Price book

Chapter 5. Doing Things Differently: Variations in State Economic Policies

55. The _____, 1949-1991, was an economic organization of communist states and a kind of Eastern Bloc equivalent to--but more geographically inclusive than--the European Economic Community. The military equivalent to the Comecon was the Warsaw Pact, though Comecon's membership was significantly wider. The Comecon was the Eastern Bloc's reply to the formation of the OEEC.

   a. 100-year flood
   b. 1921 recession
   c. 130-30 fund
   d. Council for Mutual Economic Assistance

56. The term microeconomic reform (or often just _____) refers to policies directed to achieve improvements in economic efficiency, either by removing distortions in individual sectors of the economy or by reforming economy-wide policies such as tax policy and competition policy with an emphasis on economic efficiency (rather than other goals such as equity or employment growth.)

   _____ usually refers to government action to improve efficiency in economic markets to overcome regulatory and statutory impediments. It may sometimes also refer to legislative efforts to reduce the size of government, in order to improve economic efficiency.

   a. Inventory analysis
   b. Isocost
   c. Incentive
   d. Economic reform

Chapter 6. Transnational Corporations: The Primary Movers and Shapers of the Global Economy

1. The _____ consists of a number of economic theories which describe the nature of the firm, company including its existence, its behaviour, and its relationship with the market.

In simplified terms, the _____ aims to answer these questions:

1. Existence - why do firms emerge, why are not all transactions in the economy mediated over the market?
2. Boundaries - why the boundary between firms and the market is located exactly there? Which transactions are performed internally and which are negotiated on the market?
3. Organization - why are firms structured in such specific way? What is the interplay of formal and informal relationships?

Despite looking simple, these questions are not answered by the established economic theory, which usually views firms as given, and treats them as black boxes without any internal structure.

The First World War period saw a change of emphasis in economic theory away from industry-level analysis which mainly included analysing markets to analysis at the level of the firm, as it became increasingly clear that perfect competition was no longer an adequate model of how firms behaved. Economic theory till then had focussed on trying to understand markets alone and there had been little study on understanding why firms or organisations exist.

 a. Technology gap
 b. Policy Ineffectiveness Proposition
 c. Khazzoom-Brookes postulate
 d. Theory of the firm

2. _____ in its classic form is defined as a company from one country making a physical investment into building a factory in another country. It is the establishment of an enterprise by a foreigner. Its definition can be extended to include investments made to acquire lasting interest in enterprises operating outside of the economy of the investor.
 a. Financial Stability Forum
 b. Foreign direct investment
 c. Non-governmental organization
 d. Federal Deposit Insurance Corporation

3. In finance, _____ is investment originating from other countries. See Foreign direct investment.
 a. Preclusive purchasing
 b. Demand side economics
 c. Foreign investment
 d. Horizontal merger

4. _____ is a type of trade policy that allows traders to act and transact without interference from government. Thus, the policy permits trading partners mutual gains from trade, with goods and services produced according to the theory of comparative advantage.

Under a _____ policy, prices are a reflection of true supply and demand, and are the sole determinant of resource allocation.

 a. 100-year flood
 b. 130-30 fund
 c. 1921 recession
 d. Free Trade

5. _____ is the political philosophy and practice derived from the work of Karl Marx and Friedrich Engels. _____ holds at its core a critical analysis of capitalism and a theory of social change. The powerful and innovative methods of analysis introduced by Marx have been very influential in a broad range of disciplines.

Chapter 6. Transnational Corporations: The Primary Movers and Shapers of the Global Economy

a. Adam Smith
b. Neo-Gramscianism
c. Karl Heinrich Marx
d. Marxism

6. _____s is the social science that studies the production, distribution, and consumption of goods and services. The term _____s comes from the Ancient Greek οἰκονομῑα from οἶκος (oikos, 'house') + νόμος (nomos, 'custom' or 'law'), hence 'rules of the house(hold)'. Current _____ models developed out of the broader field of political economy in the late 19th century, owing to a desire to use an empirical approach more akin to the physical sciences.
   a. Opportunity cost
   b. Inflation
   c. Energy economics
   d. Economic

7. In economics, an _____ is any good or commodity, transported from one country to another country in a legitimate fashion, typically for use in trade. _____ goods or services are provided to foreign consumers by domestic producers. _____ is an important part of international trade.
   a. Export
   b. AD-IA Model
   c. ACCRA Cost of Living Index
   d. ACEA agreement

8. Often a characteristic of new markets and industries, _____ occurs when technologies or offerings are so new that standards and rules are in flux, resulting in competitive advantages that cannot be sustained. In response, companies must constantly compete in price or quality, or innovate in supply chain management, new value creation, or have enough financial capital to outlast other competitors.

This phenomenon is described in Richard D'Avenie;s book of the same name.

   a. Bequest motive
   b. Real prices and ideal prices
   c. Theory of the firm
   d. Hypercompetition

9. The _____ is an international organization that oversees the global financial system by following the macroeconomic policies of its member countries, in particular those with an impact on exchange rates and the balance of payments. It is an organization formed to stabilize international exchange rates and facilitate development. It also offers financial and technical assistance to its members, making it an international lender of last resort.
   a. ACCRA Cost of Living Index
   b. Office of Thrift Supervision
   c. ACEA agreement
   d. International Monetary Fund

10. In business and accounting, _____ are everything of value that is owned by a person or company. It is a claim on the property your income of a borrower. The balance sheet of a firm records the monetary value of the _____ owned by the firm.
    a. Amortization schedule
    b. Assets
    c. ACCRA Cost of Living Index
    d. ACEA agreement

11. In microeconomics, _____ is quite simply the conversion of inputs into outputs. It is an economic process that uses resources to create a good or service that is suitable for exchange. This can include manufacturing, storing, shipping, and packaging.
    a. MET
    b. Solved
    c. Red Guards
    d. Production

Chapter 6. Transnational Corporations: The Primary Movers and Shapers of the Global Economy

12. _____ Management is the succession of strategies used by management as a product goes through its _____. The conditions in which a product is sold changes over time and must be managed as it moves through its succession of stages.

The _____ goes through many phases, involves many professional disciplines, and requires many skills, tools and processes.

   a. Tax profit
   b. Corporate tax
   c. Procurement
   d. Product life cycle

13. In statistics, the _____ problem occurs when one considers a set of statistical inferences simultaneously. Errors in inference, including confidence intervals that fail to include their corresponding population parameters are more likely to occur when one considers the family as a whole. Several statistical techniques have been developed to prevent this from happening, allowing significance levels for single and _____ to be directly compared.

   a. False discovery rate
   b. Multiple comparisons
   c. Familywise error rate
   d. Hypotheses suggested by the data

14. _____ has been viewed as a process of increasing involvement of enterprises in international markets, although there is no agreed definition of _____ or international entrepreneurship. There are several _____ theories which try to explain why there are international activities.

Adam Smith claimed that a country should specialise in, and export, commodities in which it had an absolute advantage.

   a. Economic problem
   b. Internationalization
   c. Unified growth theory
   d. Uppsala model

15. _____ is the corporate management term for the act of reorganizing the legal, ownership, operational or better organized for its present needs. Alternate reasons for restructing include a change of ownership or ownership structure, demerger repositioning debt _____ and financial _____.

   a. Securitization
   b. Restructuring
   c. Forecast period
   d. Market value

16. A _____ is the investment in a manufacturing, office, or other physical company-related structure or group of structures in an area where no previous facilities exist. The name comes from the idea of building a facility literally on a 'green' field, such as farmland or a forest. Over time the term has become more metaphoric.

   a. Greenfield investment
   b. Harbert Management Corporation
   c. Master-feeder
   d. Laddering

Chapter 6. Transnational Corporations: The Primary Movers and Shapers of the Global Economy

17. Economics:

    - _____, the desire to own something and the ability to pay for it
    - _____ curve, a graphic representation of a _____ schedule
    - _____ deposit, the money in checking accounts
    - _____ pull theory, the theory that inflation occurs when _____ for goods and services exceeds existing supplies
    - _____ schedule, a table that lists the quantity of a good a person will buy it each different price
    - _____ side economics, the school of economics at believes government spending and tax cuts open economy by raising _____

    a. Variability
    c. Demand

    b. McKesson ' Robbins scandal
    d. Production

18. _____ is any long-term change in the patterns of average weather of a specific region or the Earth as a whole. _____ reflects abnormal variations to the Earth's climate and subsequent effects on other parts of the Earth, such as in the ice caps over durations ranging from decades to millions of years.

    In recent usage, especially in the context of environmental policy, _____ usually refers to changes in modern climate

    a. Climate Change
    c. 130-30 fund

    b. 1921 recession
    d. 100-year flood

19. The _____ is a protocol to the United Nations Framework Convention on Climate Change (UNFCCC or FCCC), an international environmental treaty produced at the United Nations Conference on treaty is intended to achieve 'stabilization of greenhouse gas concentrations in the atmosphere at a level that would prevent dangerous anthropogenic interference with the climate system.' The _____ establishes legally binding commitments for the reduction of four greenhouse gases (carbon dioxide, methane, nitrous oxide, sulphur hexafluoride), and two groups of gases (hydrofluorocarbons and perfluorocarbons) produced by 'Annex I' (industrialized) nations, as well as general commitments for all member countries. As of January 14 2009, 183 parties have ratified the protocol, which was initially adopted for use on 11 December 1997 in Kyoto, Japan and which entered into force on 16 February 2005. Under Kyoto, industrialized countries agreed to reduce their collective GHG emissions by 5.2% compared to the year 1990.

    a. Greenhouse gases
    c. Green New Deal

    b. Kyoto Protocol
    d. Carbon offset

20. A _____ or labor union is an organization of workers who have banded together to achieve common goals in key areas and working conditions. The _____, through its leadership, bargains with the employer on behalf of union members (rank and file members) and negotiates labor contracts (Collective bargaining) with employers. This may include the negotiation of wages, work rules, complaint procedures, rules governing hiring, firing and promotion of workers, benefits, workplace safety and policies.

    a. Trade union
    c. Guaranteed investment contracts

    b. Case-Shiller Home Price Indices
    d. Consumer goods

Chapter 6. Transnational Corporations: The Primary Movers and Shapers of the Global Economy

21. In finance, the _____s between two currencies specifies how much one currency is worth in terms of the other. It is the value of a foreign natione;s currency in terms of the home natione;s currency. For example an _____ of 102 Japanese yen to the United States dollar means that JPY 102 is worth the same as USD 1.
    a. Exchange rate
    b. ACEA agreement
    c. Interbank market
    d. ACCRA Cost of Living Index

22. A _____ is an operator or function that can either be applied to other operators (i.e. one or more of its operands or arguments are itself operators) or yield operators as result, or both. It is thus essentially the same as a higher-order function, although the syntax may be more reminiscent of (pre-, post-, or infix) operators applied to operands, rather than function application in the lambda calculus tradition. Examples of _____s are function composition, construction, and apply-to-all, but there are numerous others.
    a. 100-year flood
    b. Rebound effect
    c. 130-30 fund
    d. Functional form

23. The _____ was negotiated between members of the Organisation for Economic Co-operation and Development (OECD) between 1995 and 1998. Its purpose was to develop multilateral rules that would ensure international investment was governed in a more systematic and uniform way between states. When the first draft was leaked to the public in 1997, it drew widespread criticism from civil society groups and developing countries, particularly over the possibility that the agreement would make it difficult to regulate foreign investors.
    a. Market access
    b. Bilateral Investment Treaty
    c. Multilateral Agreement on Investment
    d. Trade barrier

24. A _____ or transnational corporation is a corporation or enterprise that manages production or delivers services in more than one country. It can also be referred to as an international corporation.

The first modern MNC is generally thought to be the Dutch East India Company, established in 1602.

   a. Foreign direct investment
   b. Multinational corporation
   c. Luxembourg Income Study
   d. Rakon

25. _____ is the process by which the activities of an organization, particularly those regarding decision-making, become concentrated within a particular location and/or group.

In political science, this refers to the concentration of a government's power - both geographically and politically, into a centralized government.

   a. Teaser rate
   b. Product innovation
   c. Centralization
   d. Microcap stock

26. A _____ is a geographical region that has economic laws that are more liberal than a country's typical economic laws. The category '_____' covers a broad range of more specific zone types, including Free Trade Zones (FTZ), Export Processing Zones (EPZ), Free Zones (FZ), Industrial Estates (IE), Free Ports, Urban Enterprise Zones and others. Usually the goal of a structure is to increase foreign investment.
    a. Transfer problem
    b. Special Economic Zone
    c. Customs union
    d. Linder hypothesis

Chapter 6. Transnational Corporations: The Primary Movers and Shapers of the Global Economy

27. The _____ in Davos, Switzerland (January, 2003) triggered anti-globalization protests across Switzerland. Access to the town of Davos was blocked by the police of Grisons, with reinforcements from other cantons, and even Austrian police, which was unprecedented. On Saturday January 25, the day scheduled for a protest march in Davos, only selected protesters were allowed to pass.

   a. 130-30 fund
   b. 1921 recession
   c. 100-year flood
   d. World Economic Forum

28. _____ has several particular meanings:

   - in mathematics
     - _____ function
     - Euler _____
     - _____
     - _____ subgroup
     - method of _____ s (partial differential equations)
   - in physics and engineering
     - any _____ curve that shows the relationship between certain input- and output parameters, e.g.
     - an I-V or current-voltage _____ is the current in a circuit as a function of the applied voltage
     - Receiver-Operator _____
   - in fiction
     - in Dungeons ' Dragons, _____ is another name for ability score

   a. Russian financial crisis
   b. Demand
   c. Technocracy
   d. Characteristic

29. _____ relates to decisions that define expectations, grant power, or verify performance. It consists either of a separate process or of a specific part of management or leadership processes. Sometimes people set up a government to administer these processes and systems.

   a. 100-year flood
   b. 1921 recession
   c. 130-30 fund
   d. Governance

30. The phrase _____, according to the Organization for Economic Co-operation and Development, refers to 'creative work undertaken on a systematic basis in order to increase the stock of knowledge, including knowledge of man, culture and society, and the use of this stock of knowledge to devise new applications [sic]'

New product design and development is more than often a crucial factor in the survival of a company. In an industry that is fast changing, firms must continually revise their design and range of products. This is necessary due to continuous technology change and development as well as other competitors and the changing preference of customers.

   a. Research and development
   b. 1921 recession
   c. 100-year flood
   d. 130-30 fund

Chapter 6. Transnational Corporations: The Primary Movers and Shapers of the Global Economy

31. _____ Group is one of the largest corporate conglomerates (Keiretsu) in Japan and one of the largest publicly traded companies in the world. Surugacho (Suruga Street) (1856), from One Hundred Famous Views of Edo, by Hiroshige, depicting the Echigoya kimono and money exchange store with Mount Fuji in background. Currently, the _____ Main Building (ä¸‰äº•æœ¬é¤¨), which houses Sumitomo _____ Banking Corporation, _____ Fudosan, The Chuo _____ Trust and Banking Co.
   a. 1921 recession
   b. 130-30 fund
   c. 100-year flood
   d. Mitsui

32. A _____ is a set of companies with interlocking business relationships and shareholdings. It is a type of business group.

The prototypical _____ are those which appeared in Japan during the 'economic miracle' following World War II.

   a. 130-30 fund
   b. 1921 recession
   c. 100-year flood
   d. Keiretsu

33. _____ is a forum for 21 Pacific Rim countries (styled 'member economies') to cooperate on regional trade and investment liberalisation and facilitation. APEC's objective is to enhance economic growth and prosperity in the region and to strengthen the Asia-Pacific community. Members account for approximately 40% of the world's population, approximately 54% of world GDP and about 44% of world trade.
   a. AD-IA Model
   b. Asia-Pacific Economic Cooperation
   c. ACCRA Cost of Living Index
   d. ACEA agreement

34. A mutual _____ or stockholder is an individual or company (including a corporation) that legally owns one or more shares of stock in a joint stock company. A company's _____s collectively own that company. Thus, the typical goal of such companies is to enhance _____ value.
   a. Profit warning
   b. Relative valuation
   c. Prime Standard
   d. Shareholder

35. _____ is the a method of technical and economic research of the systems for purpose to optimize a parity between system's consumer functions or properties and expenses to achieve those functions or properties.

This methodology for continuous perfection of production, industrial technologies, organizational structures was developed by Juryj Sobolev in 1948 at the 'Perm telephone factory'

- 1948 Juryj Sobolev - the first success in application of a method analysis at the 'Perm telephone factory'.
- 1949 - the first application for the invention as result of use of the new method.

Chapter 6. Transnational Corporations: The Primary Movers and Shapers of the Global Economy

Today in economically developed countries practically each enterprise or the company use methodology of the kind of functional-cost analysis as a practice of the quality management, most full satisfying to principles of standards of series ISO 9000.

- Interest of consumer not in products itself, but the advantage which it will receive from its usage.
- The consumer aspires to reduce his expenses
- Functions needed by consumer can be executed in the various ways, and, hence, with various efficiency and expenses. Among possible alternatives of realization of functions exist such in which the parity of quality and the price is the optimal for the consumer.

The goal of _____ is achievement of the highest consumer satisfaction of production at simultaneous decrease in all kinds of industrial expenses Classical _____ has three English synonyms - Value Engineering, Value Management, Value Analysis.

a. Monopoly wage
c. Staple financing
b. Willingness to pay
d. Function cost analysis

Chapter 7. 'Webs of Enterprise': The Geography of Transnational Production Networks

1. In microeconomics, _____ is quite simply the conversion of inputs into outputs. It is an economic process that uses resources to create a good or service that is suitable for exchange. This can include manufacturing, storing, shipping, and packaging.
   a. Solved
   b. Red Guards
   c. MET
   d. Production

2. _____ is a forum for 21 Pacific Rim countries (styled 'member economies') to cooperate on regional trade and investment liberalisation and facilitation. APEC's objective is to enhance economic growth and prosperity in the region and to strengthen the Asia-Pacific community. Members account for approximately 40% of the world's population, approximately 54% of world GDP and about 44% of world trade.
   a. Asia-Pacific Economic Cooperation
   b. AD-IA Model
   c. ACCRA Cost of Living Index
   d. ACEA agreement

3. The _____ is an economic and political union of 27 member states, located primarily in Europe. It was established by the Treaty of Maastricht on 1 November 1993, upon the foundations of the pre-existing European Economic Community. With a population of almost 500 million, the _____ generates an estimated 30% share (US$18.4 trillion in 2008) of the nominal gross world product.
   a. ACCRA Cost of Living Index
   b. ACEA agreement
   c. European Union
   d. European Court of Justice

4. The _____ is a trilateral trade bloc in North America created by the governments of the United States, Canada, and Mexico. The agreement creating the trade bloc came into force on January 1, 1994. It superseded the Canada-United States Free Trade Agreement between the U.S. and Canada.
   a. Case-Shiller Home Price Indices
   b. Demand-side technologies
   c. Federal Reserve Bank Notes
   d. North American Free Trade Agreement

5. _____ according to Onuoha (2007) is the practice of starting new organizations or revitalizing mature organizations, particularly new businesses generally in response to identified opportunities. _____ is often a difficult undertaking, as a vast majority of new businesses fail. Entrepreneurial activities are substantially different depending on the type of organization that is being started.
   a. Entrepreneurship
   b. Intrapreneurship
   c. ACEA agreement
   d. ACCRA Cost of Living Index

6. The phrase _____, according to the Organization for Economic Co-operation and Development, refers to 'creative work undertaken on a systematic basis in order to increase the stock of knowledge, including knowledge of man, culture and society, and the use of this stock of knowledge to devise new applications [sic]'

   New product design and development is more than often a crucial factor in the survival of a company. In an industry that is fast changing, firms must continually revise their design and range of products. This is necessary due to continuous technology change and development as well as other competitors and the changing preference of customers.

   a. Research and development
   b. 1921 recession
   c. 100-year flood
   d. 130-30 fund

Chapter 7. `Webs of Enterprise`: The Geography of Transnational Production Networks

7. _____ has been viewed as a process of increasing involvement of enterprises in international markets, although there is no agreed definition of _____ or international entrepreneurship. There are several _____ theories which try to explain why there are international activities.

Adam Smith claimed that a country should specialise in, and export, commodities in which it had an absolute advantage.

- a. Uppsala model
- b. Unified growth theory
- c. Economic problem
- d. Internationalization

8. _____s is the social science that studies the production, distribution, and consumption of goods and services. The term _____s comes from the Ancient Greek οἰκονομῑα from οἶκος (oikos, 'house') + νόμος (nomos, 'custom' or 'law'), hence 'rules of the house(hold)'. Current _____ models developed out of the broader field of political economy in the late 19th century, owing to a desire to use an empirical approach more akin to the physical sciences.

- a. Energy economics
- b. Opportunity cost
- c. Inflation
- d. Economic

9. A _____ is a geographical region that has economic laws that are more liberal than a country's typical economic laws. The category '_____' covers a broad range of more specific zone types, including Free Trade Zones (FTZ), Export Processing Zones (EPZ), Free Zones (FZ), Industrial Estates (IE), Free Ports, Urban Enterprise Zones and others. Usually the goal of a structure is to increase foreign investment.

- a. Special Economic Zone
- b. Transfer problem
- c. Linder hypothesis
- d. Customs union

10. The _____ consists of a number of economic theories which describe the nature of the firm, company including its existence, its behaviour, and its relationship with the market.

In simplified terms, the _____ aims to answer these questions:

1. Existence - why do firms emerge, why are not all transactions in the economy mediated over the market?
2. Boundaries - why the boundary between firms and the market is located exactly there? Which transactions are performed internally and which are negotiated on the market?
3. Organization - why are firms structured in such specific way? What is the interplay of formal and informal relationships?

Despite looking simple, these questions are not answered by the established economic theory, which usually views firms as given, and treats them as black boxes without any internal structure.

The First World War period saw a change of emphasis in economic theory away from industry-level analysis which mainly included analysing markets to analysis at the level of the firm, as it became increasingly clear that perfect competition was no longer an adequate model of how firms behaved. Economic theory till then had focussed on trying to understand markets alone and there had been little study on understanding why firms or organisations exist.

Chapter 7. `Webs of Enterprise`: The Geography of Transnational Production Networks

a. Technology gap
c. Khazzoom-Brookes postulate
b. Policy Ineffectiveness Proposition
d. Theory of the firm

11. In finance, _____ is investment originating from other countries. See Foreign direct investment.
    a. Demand side economics
    b. Preclusive purchasing
    c. Foreign investment
    d. Horizontal merger

12. A _____ is a duty imposed on goods when they are moved across a political boundary. They are usually associated with protectionism, the economic policy of restraining trade between nations. For political reasons, _____s are usually imposed on imported goods, although they may also be imposed on exported goods.
    a. 130-30 fund
    b. 100-year flood
    c. 1921 recession
    d. Tariff

13. _____ is the corporate management term for the act of reorganizing the legal, ownership, operational or better organized for its present needs. Alternate reasons for restructing include a change of ownership or ownership structure, demerger repositioning debt _____ and financial _____.
    a. Forecast period
    b. Market value
    c. Securitization
    d. Restructuring

14. _____, sometimes referred to as divestment, refers to the use of a concerted economic boycott, with specific emphasis on liquidating stock, to pressure a government, industry or in the case of govennments, even regime change. The term was first used in the 1980s, most commonly in the United States, to refer to the use of a concerted economic boycott designed to pressure the government of South Africa into abolishing its policy of apartheid. The term has also been applied to actions targeting Iran, Sudan, Northern Ireland, Myanmar, and Israel.
    a. 100-year flood
    b. 1921 recession
    c. 130-30 fund
    d. Disinvestment

15. A _____ is the investment in a manufacturing, office, or other physical company-related structure or group of structures in an area where no previous facilities exist. The name comes from the idea of building a facility literally on a 'green' field, such as farmland or a forest. Over time the term has become more metaphoric.
    a. Harbert Management Corporation
    b. Master-feeder
    c. Laddering
    d. Greenfield investment

16. In economics and business decision-making, _____ are costs that cannot be recovered once they have been incurred. _____ are sometimes contrasted with variable costs, which are the costs that will change due to the proposed course of action, and prospective costs which are costs that will be incurred if an action is taken.

In traditional microeconomic theory, only variable costs are relevant to a decision.

    a. Hyperbolic discounting
    b. Post-purchase rationalization
    c. Halo effect
    d. Sunk costs

17. _____s are a type of administrative division, in some countries managed by a local government. They vary greatly in size, spanning entire regions or counties, several municipalities, or subdivisions of municipalities.

In Austria, a _____ or Bezirk is an administrative division normally encompassing several municipalities, roughly equivalent to the Landkreis in Germany.

   a. District
   c. 100-year flood
   b. 1921 recession
   d. 130-30 fund

18. A _____ is an entity formed between two or more parties to undertake economic activity together. The parties agree to create a new entity by both contributing equity, and they then share in the revenues, expenses, and control of the enterprise. The venture can be for one specific project only, or a continuing business relationship such as the Fuji Xerox _____.
   a. Joint venture
   c. Property right
   b. Nexus of contracts
   d. Business valuation

19. An _____ is a person who has possession of an enterprise and assumes significant accountability for the inherent risks and the outcome. It is an ambitious leader who combines land, labor, and capital to create and market new goods or services. The term is a loanword from French and was first defined by the Irish economist Richard Cantillon.
   a. Expansionary policies
   c. ACCRA Cost of Living Index
   b. Entrepreneur
   d. ACEA agreement

20. In economics, an _____ is any good or commodity, transported from one country to another country in a legitimate fashion, typically for use in trade. _____ goods or services are provided to foreign consumers by domestic producers. _____ is an important part of international trade.
   a. ACEA agreement
   c. AD-IA Model
   b. ACCRA Cost of Living Index
   d. Export

21. _____ is a Regional Trade Agreement among Argentina, Brazil, Paraguay and Uruguay founded in 1991 by the Treaty of Asunci>ón, which was later amended and updated by the 1994 Treaty of Ouro Preto. Its purpose is to promote free trade and the fluid movement of goods, people, and currency.

_____ origins trace back to 1985 when Presidents Ra>úl Alfons>ín of Argentina and Jos>é Sarney of Brazil signed the Argentina-Brazil Integration and Economics Cooperation Program or PICE .

   a. Free trade area
   c. 130-30 fund
   b. 100-year flood
   d. MERCOSUR

22. The phrase _____ and acquisitions refers to the aspect of corporate strategy, corporate finance and management dealing with the buying, selling and combining of different companies that can aid, finance, or help a growing company in a given industry grow rapidly without having to create another business entity.

An acquisition, also known as a takeover or a buyout, is the buying of one company (the 'target') by another. An acquisition may be friendly or hostile.

   a. Differential accumulation
   c. Political economy
   b. Peace dividend
   d. Mergers

Chapter 7. `Webs of Enterprise`: The Geography of Transnational Production Networks

23. _____ is an offer (often competitive) of setting a price one is willing to pay for something. A price offer is called a bid. The term may be used in context of auctions, stock exchange, card games, or real estate transactions.
    a. Bidding
    b. Central limit order book
    c. Normal good
    d. Bord halfpenny

24. _____ is a type of trade policy that allows traders to act and transact without interference from government. Thus, the policy permits trading partners mutual gains from trade, with goods and services produced according to the theory of comparative advantage.

Under a _____ policy, prices are a reflection of true supply and demand, and are the sole determinant of resource allocation.

   a. Free Trade
   b. 1921 recession
   c. 100-year flood
   d. 130-30 fund

Chapter 8. Dynamics of Conflict and Collaboration: Both Transnational Corporations

1. _____ is a forum for 21 Pacific Rim countries (styled 'member economies') to cooperate on regional trade and investment liberalisation and facilitation. APEC's objective is to enhance economic growth and prosperity in the region and to strengthen the Asia-Pacific community. Members account for approximately 40% of the world's population, approximately 54% of world GDP and about 44% of world trade.

   a. ACEA agreement
   b. AD-IA Model
   c. ACCRA Cost of Living Index
   d. Asia-Pacific Economic Cooperation

2. The _____ is an economic and political union of 27 member states, located primarily in Europe. It was established by the Treaty of Maastricht on 1 November 1993, upon the foundations of the pre-existing European Economic Community. With a population of almost 500 million, the _____ generates an estimated 30% share (US$18.4 trillion in 2008) of the nominal gross world product.

   a. ACCRA Cost of Living Index
   b. European Union
   c. ACEA agreement
   d. European Court of Justice

3. The _____ is a trilateral trade bloc in North America created by the governments of the United States, Canada, and Mexico. The agreement creating the trade bloc came into force on January 1, 1994. It superseded the Canada-United States Free Trade Agreement between the U.S. and Canada.

   a. Case-Shiller Home Price Indices
   b. Federal Reserve Bank Notes
   c. North American Free Trade Agreement
   d. Demand-side technologies

4. In economics and finance, _____ is the practice of taking advantage of a price differential between two or more markets: striking a combination of matching deals that capitalize upon the imbalance, the profit being the difference between the market prices. When used by academics, an _____ is a transaction that involves no negative cash flow at any probabilistic or temporal state and a positive cash flow in at least one state; in simple terms, a risk-free profit. A person who engages in _____ is called an arbitrageur--such as a bank or brokerage firm.

   a. Options Price Reporting Authority
   b. Alternext
   c. Electronic trading
   d. Arbitrage

5. _____ is the removal or simplification of government rules and regulations that constrain the operation of market forces. _____ does not mean elimination of laws against fraud, but eliminating or reducing government control of how business is done, thereby moving toward a more free market.

   The stated rationale for '_____' is often that fewer and simpler regulations will lead to a raised level of competitiveness, therefore higher productivity, more efficiency and lower prices overall.

   a. Secular basis
   b. Deregulation
   c. Macroeconomic policy instruments
   d. Fundamental psychological law

6. A _____ is the investment in a manufacturing, office, or other physical company-related structure or group of structures in an area where no previous facilities exist. The name comes from the idea of building a facility literally on a 'green' field, such as farmland or a forest. Over time the term has become more metaphoric.

   a. Master-feeder
   b. Harbert Management Corporation
   c. Laddering
   d. Greenfield investment

7. _____ is a type of trade policy that allows traders to act and transact without interference from government. Thus, the policy permits trading partners mutual gains from trade, with goods and services produced according to the theory of comparative advantage.

Chapter 8. Dynamics of Conflict and Collaboration: Both Transnational Corporations 53

Under a _____ policy, prices are a reflection of true supply and demand, and are the sole determinant of resource allocation.

a. 100-year flood
c. Free Trade
b. 1921 recession
d. 130-30 fund

8. In economics, the _____ measures the payments that flow between any individual country and all other countries. It is used to summarize all international economic transactions for that country during a specific time period, usually a year. The _____ is determined by the country's exports and imports of goods, services, and financial capital, as well as financial transfers.

a. Skyscraper Index
c. Gross domestic product per barrel
b. Balance of payments
d. Gross world product

9. A _____ is the transfer of wealth from one party (such as a person or company) to another. A _____ is usually made in exchange for the provision of goods, services or both, or to fulfill a legal obligation.

The simplest and oldest form of _____ is barter, the exchange of one good or service for another.

a. Social gravity
c. Going concern
b. Soft count
d. Payment

10. _____ is one of the four Ps of the marketing mix. The other three aspects are product, promotion, and place. It is also a key variable in microeconomic price allocation theory.

a. Point of total assumption
c. Pricing
b. Premium pricing
d. Guaranteed Maximum Price

11. The phrase _____, according to the Organization for Economic Co-operation and Development, refers to 'creative work undertaken on a systematic basis in order to increase the stock of knowledge, including knowledge of man, culture and society, and the use of this stock of knowledge to devise new applications [sic]'

New product design and development is more than often a crucial factor in the survival of a company. In an industry that is fast changing, firms must continually revise their design and range of products. This is necessary due to continuous technology change and development as well as other competitors and the changing preference of customers.

a. Research and development
c. 100-year flood
b. 1921 recession
d. 130-30 fund

12. _____ refers to the pricing of contributions (assets, tangible and intangible, services, and funds) transferred within an organization. For example, goods from the production division may be sold to the marketing division, or goods from a parent company may be sold to a foreign subsidiary. Since the prices are set within an organization (i.e. controlled), the typical market mechanisms that establish prices for such transactions between third parties may not apply.

a. San Francisco congestion pricing
c. Two-part tariff
b. Rational pricing
d. Transfer pricing

Chapter 8. Dynamics of Conflict and Collaboration: Both Transnational Corporations

13. In finance, _____ is investment originating from other countries. See Foreign direct investment.
    a. Preclusive purchasing
    b. Horizontal merger
    c. Demand side economics
    d. Foreign investment

14. _____ is the process of sharing of skills, knowledge, technologies, methods of manufacturing, samples of manufacturing and facilities among governments and other institutions to ensure that scientific and technological developments are accessible to a wider range of users who can then further develop and exploit the technology into new products, processes, applications, materials or services. It is closely related to (and may arguably be considered a subset of) Knowledge transfer. Related terms, used almost synonymously, include 'technology valorisation' and 'technology commercialisation'.
    a. Technology transfer
    b. Patent
    c. Law of increasing relative cost
    d. Judgment summons

15. _____ ndustrialization in North America, is the process of social and economic change whereby a human group is transformed from a pre-industrial society into an industrial one. _____ t is a part of a wider modernisation process, where social change and economic development are closely related with technological innovation, particularly with the development of large-scale energy and metallurgy production. _____ t is the extensive organisation of an economy for the purpose of manufacturing.
    a. ACCRA Cost of Living Index
    b. ACEA agreement
    c. AD-IA Model
    d. Industrialization

16. In microeconomics, _____ is quite simply the conversion of inputs into outputs. It is an economic process that uses resources to create a good or service that is suitable for exchange. This can include manufacturing, storing, shipping, and packaging.
    a. MET
    b. Solved
    c. Red Guards
    d. Production

17. _____ is the term denoting either an entrance or changes which are inserted into a system and which activate/modify a process. It is an abstract concept, used in the modeling, system(s) design and system(s) exploitation. It is usually connected with other terms, e.g., _____ field, _____ variable, _____ parameter, _____ value, _____ signal, _____ device and _____ file.
    a. ACCRA Cost of Living Index
    b. AD-IA Model
    c. ACEA agreement
    d. Input

18. _____ refers to a business or organization attempting to acquire goods or services to accomplish the goals of the enterprise. Though there are several organizations that attempt to set standards in the _____ process, processes can vary greatly between organizations. Typically the word '_____' is not used interchangeably with the word 'procurement', since procurement typically includes Expediting, Supplier Quality, and Traffic and Logistics (T'L) in addition to _____.
    a. 100-year flood
    b. 130-30 fund
    c. Free port
    d. Purchasing

19. In economics, an _____ is any good or commodity, transported from one country to another country in a legitimate fashion, typically for use in trade. _____ goods or services are provided to foreign consumers by domestic producers. _____ is an important part of international trade.

a. Export
b. ACCRA Cost of Living Index
c. ACEA agreement
d. AD-IA Model

20. _____ according to Onuoha (2007) is the practice of starting new organizations or revitalizing mature organizations, particularly new businesses generally in response to identified opportunities. _____ is often a difficult undertaking, as a vast majority of new businesses fail. Entrepreneurial activities are substantially different depending on the type of organization that is being started.

a. Entrepreneurship
b. ACEA agreement
c. Intrapreneurship
d. ACCRA Cost of Living Index

21. _____ is any long-term change in the patterns of average weather of a specific region or the Earth as a whole. _____ reflects abnormal variations to the Earth's climate and subsequent effects on other parts of the Earth, such as in the ice caps over durations ranging from decades to millions of years.

In recent usage, especially in the context of environmental policy, _____ usually refers to changes in modern climate

a. 1921 recession
b. 130-30 fund
c. 100-year flood
d. Climate Change

22. The _____ is a protocol to the United Nations Framework Convention on Climate Change (UNFCCC or FCCC), an international environmental treaty produced at the United Nations Conference on treaty is intended to achieve 'stabilization of greenhouse gas concentrations in the atmosphere at a level that would prevent dangerous anthropogenic interference with the climate system.' The _____ establishes legally binding commitments for the reduction of four greenhouse gases (carbon dioxide, methane, nitrous oxide, sulphur hexafluoride), and two groups of gases (hydrofluorocarbons and perfluorocarbons) produced by 'Annex I' (industrialized) nations, as well as general commitments for all member countries. As of January 14 2009, 183 parties have ratified the protocol, which was initially adopted for use on 11 December 1997 in Kyoto, Japan and which entered into force on 16 February 2005. Under Kyoto, industrialized countries agreed to reduce their collective GHG emissions by 5.2% compared to the year 1990.

a. Green New Deal
b. Kyoto Protocol
c. Carbon offset
d. Greenhouse gases

23. The field of _____ looks at the relationship between management and workers, particularly groups of workers represented by a union.

Labor relations is an important factor in analyzing 'varieties of capitalism', such as neocorporatism, social democracy, and neoliberalism

Labor relations can take place on many levels, such as the 'shop-floor', the regional level, and the national level.

a. AD-IA Model
b. Industrial relations
c. ACEA agreement
d. ACCRA Cost of Living Index

24. A _____ or labor union is an organization of workers who have banded together to achieve common goals in key areas and working conditions. The _____, through its leadership, bargains with the employer on behalf of union members (rank and file members) and negotiates labor contracts (Collective bargaining) with employers. This may include the negotiation of wages, work rules, complaint procedures, rules governing hiring, firing and promotion of workers, benefits, workplace safety and policies.
- a. Guaranteed investment contracts
- b. Case-Shiller Home Price Indices
- c. Trade union
- d. Consumer goods

25. In economics, an _____ is any good (e.g. a commodity) or service brought into one country from another country in a legitimate fashion, typically for use in trade.It is a good that is brought in from another country for sale. _____ goods or services are provided to domestic consumers by foreign producers. An _____ in the receiving country is an export to the sending country.
- a. Economic integration
- b. Import quota
- c. Import
- d. Incoterms

26. A _____ is a place of residence or refuge and comfort. It is usually a place in which an individual or a family can rest and be able to store personal property. Most modern-day households contain sanitary facilities and a means of preparing food.
- a. 100-year flood
- b. 1921 recession
- c. Home
- d. 130-30 fund

27. _____ is an offer (often competitive) of setting a price one is willing to pay for something. A price offer is called a bid. The term may be used in context of auctions, stock exchange, card games, or real estate transactions.
- a. Normal good
- b. Bord halfpenny
- c. Central limit order book
- d. Bidding

28. _____ is the acquisition of goods and/or services at the best possible total cost of ownership, in the right quantity and quality, at the right time, in the right place and from the right source for the direct benefit or use of corporations or individuals, generally via a contract. Simple _____ may involve nothing more than repeat purchasing. Complex _____ could involve finding long term partners - or even 'co-destiny' suppliers that might fundamentally commit one organization to another.
- a. Sole proprietorship
- b. Golden umbrella
- c. Pre-emerging markets
- d. Procurement

29. _____ in economics and business is the result of an exchange and from that trade we assign a numerical monetary value to a good, service or asset. If Alice trades Bob 4 apples for an orange, the _____ of an orange is 4 apples. Inversely, the _____ of an apple is 1/4 oranges.
- a. Price war
- b. Premium pricing
- c. Price
- d. Price book

Chapter 9. `Fabricating Fashion`: The Textiles and Garments Industries 57

1. The _____ was a period in the late 18th and early 19th centuries when major changes in agriculture, manufacturing, mining, and transportation had a profound effect on the socioeconomic and cultural conditions in Britain. The changes subsequently spread throughout Europe, North America, and eventually the world. The onset of the _____ marked a major turning point in human society; almost every aspect of daily life was eventually influenced in some way.
   a. Adolf Hitler
   b. Adam Smith
   c. Adolph Fischer
   d. Industrial Revolution

2. The _____ movement is movement of movements which are critical of the globalization of capitalism. Participants base their criticisms on a number of related ideas. What is shared is that participants stand in opposition to the unregulated political power of large, multi-national corporations and to the powers exercised through trade agreements.
   a. Anti-consumerism
   b. Asset price inflation
   c. Anti-globalization
   d. Overcapitalisation

3. _____ is that which is owed; usually referencing assets owed, but the term can also cover moral obligations and other interactions not requiring money. In the case of assets, _____ is a means of using future purchasing power in the present before a summation has been earned. Some companies and corporations use _____ as a part of their overall corporate finance strategy.
   a. Debt
   b. Debenture
   c. Hard money loan
   d. Collateral Management

4. In economics, an _____ is any good or commodity, transported from one country to another country in a legitimate fashion, typically for use in trade. _____ goods or services are provided to foreign consumers by domestic producers. _____ is an important part of international trade.
   a. AD-IA Model
   b. ACEA agreement
   c. Export
   d. ACCRA Cost of Living Index

5. The _____ is a term used for industries primarily concerned with the design or manufacture of clothing as well as the distribution and use of textiles.

Prior to the manufacturing processes were mechanized, textiles were produced in the home, and excess sold for extra money. Most cloth was made from either wool, cotton, or flax, depending on the era and location.

   a. 100-year flood
   b. 130-30 fund
   c. Textile manufacture during the Industrial Revolution
   d. Textile industry

6. In microeconomics, _____ is quite simply the conversion of inputs into outputs. It is an economic process that uses resources to create a good or service that is suitable for exchange. This can include manufacturing, storing, shipping, and packaging.
   a. Solved
   b. MET
   c. Red Guards
   d. Production

7. _____ is a comparative concept of the ability and performance of a firm, sub-sector or country to sell and supply goods and/or services in a given market. Although widely used in economics and business management, the usefulness of the concept, particularly in the context of national _____, is vigorously disputed by economists, such as Paul Krugman .

The term may also be applied to markets, where it is used to refer to the extent to which the market structure may be regarded as perfectly competitive.

Chapter 9. `Fabricating Fashion`: The Textiles and Garments Industries

   a. Quota share
   c. Competitiveness
   b. Countervailing duties
   d. Debt moratorium

8. _____s is the social science that studies the production, distribution, and consumption of goods and services. The term _____s comes from the Ancient Greek οἰκονομία from οἶκος (oikos, 'house') + νόμος (nomos, 'custom' or 'law'), hence 'rules of the house(hold)'. Current _____ models developed out of the broader field of political economy in the late 19th century, owing to a desire to use an empirical approach more akin to the physical sciences.
   a. Opportunity cost
   c. Energy economics
   b. Inflation
   d. Economic

9. A _____ is a geographical region that has economic laws that are more liberal than a country's typical economic laws. The category '_____' covers a broad range of more specific zone types, including Free Trade Zones (FTZ), Export Processing Zones (EPZ), Free Zones (FZ), Industrial Estates (IE), Free Ports, Urban Enterprise Zones and others. Usually the goal of a structure is to increase foreign investment.
   a. Linder hypothesis
   c. Customs union
   b. Transfer problem
   d. Special Economic Zone

10. In finance, _____ is investment originating from other countries. See Foreign direct investment.
   a. Preclusive purchasing
   c. Horizontal merger
   b. Demand side economics
   d. Foreign investment

11. Economics:

- _____,the desire to own something and the ability to pay for it
- _____ curve, a graphic representation of a _____ schedule
- _____ deposit, the money in checking accounts
- _____ pull theory, the theory that inflation occurs when _____ for goods and services exceeds existing supplies
- _____ schedule, a table that lists the quantity of a good a person will buy it each different price
- _____ side economics, the school of economics at believes government spending and tax cuts open economy by raising _____

   a. Production
   c. Variability
   b. Demand
   d. McKesson ' Robbins scandal

12. _____ is a broad label that refers to any individuals or households that use goods and services generated within the economy. The concept of a _____ is used in different contexts, so that the usage and significance of the term may vary.

Typically when business people and economists talk of _____s they are talking about person as _____, an aggregated commodity item with little individuality other than that expressed in the buy/not-buy decision.

Chapter 9. `Fabricating Fashion`: The Textiles and Garments Industries

a. 1921 recession
c. Consumer

b. 130-30 fund
d. 100-year flood

13. _____ is any long-term change in the patterns of average weather of a specific region or the Earth as a whole. _____ reflects abnormal variations to the Earth's climate and subsequent effects on other parts of the Earth, such as in the ice caps over durations ranging from decades to millions of years.

In recent usage, especially in the context of environmental policy, _____ usually refers to changes in modern climate

a. 130-30 fund
c. Climate Change

b. 1921 recession
d. 100-year flood

14. The _____ is a protocol to the United Nations Framework Convention on Climate Change (UNFCCC or FCCC), an international environmental treaty produced at the United Nations Conference on treaty is intended to achieve 'stabilization of greenhouse gas concentrations in the atmosphere at a level that would prevent dangerous anthropogenic interference with the climate system.' The _____ establishes legally binding commitments for the reduction of four greenhouse gases (carbon dioxide, methane, nitrous oxide, sulphur hexafluoride), and two groups of gases (hydrofluorocarbons and perfluorocarbons) produced by 'Annex I' (industrialized) nations, as well as general commitments for all member countries. As of January 14 2009, 183 parties have ratified the protocol, which was initially adopted for use on 11 December 1997 in Kyoto, Japan and which entered into force on 16 February 2005. Under Kyoto, industrialized countries agreed to reduce their collective GHG emissions by 5.2% compared to the year 1990.

a. Carbon offset
c. Green New Deal

b. Greenhouse gases
d. Kyoto Protocol

15. _____ is a cross-disciplinary area concerned with protecting the safety, health and welfare of people engaged in work or employment. As a secondary effect, it may also protect co-workers, family members, employers, customers, suppliers, nearby communities, and other members of the public who are impacted by the workplace environment. It may involve interactions among many subject areas, including occupational medicine, occupational (or industrial) hygiene, public health, safety engineering, chemistry, health physics, ergonomics, toxicology, epidemiology, environmental health, industrial relations, public policy, sociology, and occupational health psychology.

a. ACCRA Cost of Living Index
c. AD-IA Model

b. ACEA agreement
d. Occupational safety and health

16. _____ is a forum for 21 Pacific Rim countries (styled 'member economies') to cooperate on regional trade and investment liberalisation and facilitation. APEC's objective is to enhance economic growth and prosperity in the region and to strengthen the Asia-Pacific community. Members account for approximately 40% of the world's population, approximately 54% of world GDP and about 44% of world trade.

a. ACCRA Cost of Living Index
c. AD-IA Model

b. ACEA agreement
d. Asia-Pacific Economic Cooperation

17. The _____ is an economic and political union of 27 member states, located primarily in Europe. It was established by the Treaty of Maastricht on 1 November 1993, upon the foundations of the pre-existing European Economic Community. With a population of almost 500 million, the _____ generates an estimated 30% share (US$18.4 trillion in 2008) of the nominal gross world product.

a. ACCRA Cost of Living Index
c. ACEA agreement
b. European Union
d. European Court of Justice

18. The _____ is a trilateral trade bloc in North America created by the governments of the United States, Canada, and Mexico. The agreement creating the trade bloc came into force on January 1, 1994. It superseded the Canada-United States Free Trade Agreement between the U.S. and Canada.
   a. Federal Reserve Bank Notes
   b. Case-Shiller Home Price Indices
   c. North American Free Trade Agreement
   d. Demand-side technologies

19. A _____ is a type of business entity in which partners (owners) share with each other the profits or losses of the business _____s are often favored over corporations for taxation purposes, as the _____ structure does not generally incur a tax on profits before it is distributed to the partners (i.e. there is no dividend tax levied.) However, depending on the _____ structure and the jurisdiction in which it operates, owners of a _____ may be exposed to greater personal liability than they would as shareholders of a corporation.

   For a country-by-country listing of types of _____s, companies, etc., see Types of business entity.

   a. Partnership
   b. Due diligence
   c. Minimum wage law
   d. Feoffee

20. In economics, an _____ is any good (e.g. a commodity) or service brought into one country from another country in a legitimate fashion, typically for use in trade. It is a good that is brought in from another country for sale. _____ goods or services are provided to domestic consumers by foreign producers. An _____ in the receiving country is an export to the sending country.
   a. Incoterms
   b. Import quota
   c. Economic integration
   d. Import

21. _____ is the economic policy of restraining trade between states, through methods such as tariffs on imported goods, restrictive quotas, and a variety of other restrictive government regulations designed to discourage imports, and prevent foreign take-over of local markets and companies. This policy is closely aligned with anti-globalization, and contrasts with free trade, where government barriers to trade are kept to a minimum. The term is mostly used in the context of economics, where _____ refers to policies or doctrines which 'protect' businesses and workers within a country by restricting or regulating trade with foreign nations.
   a. Knowledge economy
   b. Digital economy
   c. Google economy
   d. Protectionism

22. The _____ commenced in September 1986 and continued until April 1994. The round, based on the General Agreement on Tariffs and Trade (GATT) ministerial meeting in Geneva (1982), was launched in Punta del Este in Uruguay (hence the name), followed by negotiations in Montreal, Geneva, Brussels, Washington, D.C., and Tokyo, with the 20 agreements finally being signed in Marrakech - the Marrakesh Agreement. The Round transformed the GATT into the World Trade Organization.
   a. AD-IA Model
   b. ACEA agreement
   c. ACCRA Cost of Living Index
   d. Uruguay Round

23. An _____ is a type of protectionist trade restriction that sets a physical limit on the quantity of a good that can be imported into a country in a given period of time. Quotas, like other trade restrictions, are used to benefit the producers of a good in a domestic economy at the expense of all consumers of the good in that economy.

Critics say quotas often lead to corruption (bribes to get a quota allocation), smuggling (circumventing a quota), and higher prices for consumers.

   a. Import quota
   b. Agreement on Agriculture
   c. Economic integration
   d. International Monetary Systems

24. A _____ is a business that is privately owned and operated, with a small number of employees and relatively low volume of sales. The legal definition of 'small' often varies by country and industry, but is generally under 100 employees in the United States and under 50 employees in the European Union. In comparison, the definition of mid-sized business by the number of employees is generally under 500 in the U.S. and 250 for the European Union.

   a. Farmshoring
   b. Procurement
   c. Cabotage
   d. Small Business

25. Economic interventionism or _____ is an action in a Market economy taken by a government, beyond the basic regulation of fraud and enforcement of contracts, in an effort to affect its own economy. Economic intervention can be aimed at a variety of political or economic objectives, such as promoting economic growth, increasing employment, raising wages, raising or reducing prices, promoting equality, managing the money supply and interest rates, increasing profits, or addressing market failures. The intervention may to direct, or indirect as in the case of indicative planning.

   a. AD-IA Model
   b. ACCRA Cost of Living Index
   c. Economic Planning
   d. ACEA agreement

26. _____, in microeconomics, are the cost advantages that a business obtains due to expansion. They are factors that cause a producere;s average cost per unit to fall as scale is increased. _____ is a long run concept and refers to reductions in unit cost as the size of a facility, or scale, increases.

   a. Isoquant
   b. Economic production quantity
   c. Underinvestment employment relationship
   d. Economies of scale

27. In statistics, the _____ problem occurs when one considers a set of statistical inferences simultaneously. Errors in inference, including confidence intervals that fail to include their corresponding population parameters are more likely to occur when one considers the family as a whole. Several statistical techniques have been developed to prevent this from happening, allowing significance levels for single and _____ to be directly compared.

   a. Familywise error rate
   b. Hypotheses suggested by the data
   c. False discovery rate
   d. Multiple comparisons

28. _____ is a type of trade policy that allows traders to act and transact without interference from government. Thus, the policy permits trading partners mutual gains from trade, with goods and services produced according to the theory of comparative advantage.

Under a _____ policy, prices are a reflection of true supply and demand, and are the sole determinant of resource allocation.

a. 1921 recession
c. 130-30 fund
b. 100-year flood
d. Free Trade

29. _____ or specialization is the specialization of cooperative labour in specific, circumscribed tasks and roles, intended to increase the productivity of labour. Historically the growth of a more and more complex _____ is closely associated with the growth of total output and trade, the rise of capitalism, and of the complexity of industrialization processes. Later, the _____ reached the level of a scientifically-based management practice with the time and motion studies associated with Taylorism.
   a. Demarcation dispute
   c. Work-life balance
   b. Division of labour
   d. Day labor

Chapter 10. `Wheels of Change`: The Automobile Industry

1. In microeconomics, _____ is quite simply the conversion of inputs into outputs. It is an economic process that uses resources to create a good or service that is suitable for exchange. This can include manufacturing, storing, shipping, and packaging.
   a. MET
   b. Production
   c. Solved
   d. Red Guards

2. _____ is a forum for 21 Pacific Rim countries (styled 'member economies') to cooperate on regional trade and investment liberalisation and facilitation. APEC's objective is to enhance economic growth and prosperity in the region and to strengthen the Asia-Pacific community. Members account for approximately 40% of the world's population, approximately 54% of world GDP and about 44% of world trade.
   a. AD-IA Model
   b. ACCRA Cost of Living Index
   c. ACEA agreement
   d. Asia-Pacific Economic Cooperation

3. Economics:

   - _____, the desire to own something and the ability to pay for it
   - _____ curve, a graphic representation of a _____ schedule
   - _____ deposit, the money in checking accounts
   - _____ pull theory, the theory that inflation occurs when _____ for goods and services exceeds existing supplies
   - _____ schedule, a table that lists the quantity of a good a person will buy it each different price
   - _____ side economics, the school of economics at believes government spending and tax cuts open economy by raising _____

   a. Variability
   b. Production
   c. McKesson ' Robbins scandal
   d. Demand

4. _____ describes a deliberate attempt to interfere with the free and fair operation of the market and create artificial, false or misleading appearances with respect to the price of a security, commodity or currency. _____ is prohibited under Section 9(a)(2) of the Securities Exchange Act of 1934, and in Australia under Section s 1041A of the Corporations Act 2001. The Act defines _____ as transactions which create an artificial price or maintain an artificial price for a tradable security.
   a. Market manipulation
   b. Net domestic product
   c. Legal monopoly
   d. Managerial economics

5. _____ refers to various social theories about production and related socio-economic phenomena. It has varying but related meanings in different fields, as well as for Marxist and non-Marxist scholars. The T-Ford became a symbol of effective mass production.
   a. Marginal rate of transformation
   b. Productivity
   c. Piece work
   d. Fordism

6. _____ is any long-term change in the patterns of average weather of a specific region or the Earth as a whole. _____ reflects abnormal variations to the Earth's climate and subsequent effects on other parts of the Earth, such as in the ice caps over durations ranging from decades to millions of years.

In recent usage, especially in the context of environmental policy, _____ usually refers to changes in modern climate

   a. Climate Change
   c. 1921 recession
   b. 100-year flood
   d. 130-30 fund

7. _____s is the social science that studies the production, distribution, and consumption of goods and services. The term _____s comes from the Ancient Greek οἰκονομία from οἶκος (oikos, 'house') + νόμος (nomos, 'custom' or 'law'), hence 'rules of the house(hold)'. Current _____ models developed out of the broader field of political economy in the late 19th century, owing to a desire to use an empirical approach more akin to the physical sciences.
   a. Inflation
   c. Economic
   b. Opportunity cost
   d. Energy economics

8. The _____ is a protocol to the United Nations Framework Convention on Climate Change (UNFCCC or FCCC), an international environmental treaty produced at the United Nations Conference on treaty is intended to achieve 'stabilization of greenhouse gas concentrations in the atmosphere at a level that would prevent dangerous anthropogenic interference with the climate system.' The _____ establishes legally binding commitments for the reduction of four greenhouse gases (carbon dioxide, methane, nitrous oxide, sulphur hexafluoride), and two groups of gases (hydrofluorocarbons and perfluorocarbons) produced by 'Annex I' (industrialized) nations, as well as general commitments for all member countries. As of January 14 2009, 183 parties have ratified the protocol, which was initially adopted for use on 11 December 1997 in Kyoto, Japan and which entered into force on 16 February 2005. Under Kyoto, industrialized countries agreed to reduce their collective GHG emissions by 5.2% compared to the year 1990.
   a. Carbon offset
   c. Green New Deal
   b. Kyoto Protocol
   d. Greenhouse gases

9. A _____ is a geographical region that has economic laws that are more liberal than a country's typical economic laws. The category '_____' covers a broad range of more specific zone types, including Free Trade Zones (FTZ), Export Processing Zones (EPZ), Free Zones (FZ), Industrial Estates (IE), Free Ports, Urban Enterprise Zones and others. Usually the goal of a structure is to increase foreign investment.
   a. Customs union
   c. Special Economic Zone
   b. Linder hypothesis
   d. Transfer problem

10. _____ is a term that is used to describe the overall process of invention, innovation and diffusion of technology or processes. The term is redundant with technological development, technological achievement, and technological progress. In essence _____ is the invention of a technology (or a process), the continuous process of improving a technology (in which it often becomes cheaper) and its diffusion throughout industry or society.
   a. 100-year flood
   c. Technological change
   b. 1921 recession
   d. 130-30 fund

11. The _____ consists of a number of economic theories which describe the nature of the firm, company including its existence, its behaviour, and its relationship with the market.

Chapter 10. `Wheels of Change`: The Automobile Industry

In simplified terms, the _____ aims to answer these questions:

1. Existence - why do firms emerge, why are not all transactions in the economy mediated over the market?
2. Boundaries - why the boundary between firms and the market is located exactly there? Which transactions are performed internally and which are negotiated on the market?
3. Organization - why are firms structured in such specific way? What is the interplay of formal and informal relationships?

Despite looking simple, these questions are not answered by the established economic theory, which usually views firms as given, and treats them as black boxes without any internal structure.

The First World War period saw a change of emphasis in economic theory away from industry-level analysis which mainly included analysing markets to analysis at the level of the firm, as it became increasingly clear that perfect competition was no longer an adequate model of how firms behaved. Economic theory till then had focussed on trying to understand markets alone and there had been little study on understanding why firms or organisations exist.

    a. Policy Ineffectiveness Proposition
    b. Khazzoom-Brookes postulate
    c. Theory of the firm
    d. Technology gap

12.   In economics, an _____ is any good (e.g. a commodity) or service brought into one country from another country in a legitimate fashion, typically for use in trade. It is a good that is brought in from another country for sale. _____ goods or services are provided to domestic consumers by foreign producers. An _____ in the receiving country is an export to the sending country.
    a. Economic integration
    b. Import
    c. Import quota
    d. Incoterms

13.   The _____ is an economic and political union of 27 member states, located primarily in Europe. It was established by the Treaty of Maastricht on 1 November 1993, upon the foundations of the pre-existing European Economic Community. With a population of almost 500 million, the _____ generates an estimated 30% share (US$18.4 trillion in 2008) of the nominal gross world product.
    a. European Union
    b. ACEA agreement
    c. ACCRA Cost of Living Index
    d. European Court of Justice

14.   _____ is any (course of) action deliberately taken (or not taken) to manage human activities with a view to prevent, reduce or mitigate harmful effects on nature and natural resources, and ensuring that man-made changes to the environment do not have harmful effects on humans.

It is useful to consider that _____ comprises two major terms: environment and policy. Environment primarily refers to the ecological (ecosystems) dimension, but can also take account of social (quality of life) dimension and an economic (resource management) dimension.

a. AD-IA Model
b. ACEA agreement
c. ACCRA Cost of Living Index
d. Environmental policy

15. In economics, an _____ is any good or commodity, transported from one country to another country in a legitimate fashion, typically for use in trade. _____ goods or services are provided to foreign consumers by domestic producers. _____ is an important part of international trade.
   a. AD-IA Model
   b. ACCRA Cost of Living Index
   c. ACEA agreement
   d. Export

16. The phrase _____ and acquisitions refers to the aspect of corporate strategy, corporate finance and management dealing with the buying, selling and combining of different companies that can aid, finance, or help a growing company in a given industry grow rapidly without having to create another business entity.

An acquisition, also known as a takeover or a buyout, is the buying of one company (the 'target') by another. An acquisition may be friendly or hostile.

   a. Peace dividend
   b. Political economy
   c. Differential accumulation
   d. Mergers

17. Economic interventionism or _____ is an action in a Market economy taken by a government, beyond the basic regulation of fraud and enforcement of contracts, in an effort to affect its own economy. Economic intervention can be aimed at a variety of political or economic objectives, such as promoting economic growth, increasing employment, raising wages, raising or reducing prices, promoting equality, managing the money supply and interest rates, increasing profits, or addressing market failures. The intervention may to direct, or indirect as in the case of indicative planning.
   a. ACCRA Cost of Living Index
   b. ACEA agreement
   c. AD-IA Model
   d. Economic Planning

18. The _____ is an international financial institution that provides financial and technical assistance to developing countries for development programs (e.g. bridges, roads, schools, etc.) with the stated goal of reducing poverty.

The _____ differs from the _____ Group, in that the _____ comprises only two institutions:

- International Bank for Reconstruction and Development (IBRD)
- International Development Association (IDA)

Whereas the latter incorporates these two in addition to three more:

- International Finance Corporation (IFC)
- Multilateral Investment Guarantee Agency (MIGA)
- International Centre for Settlement of Investment Disputes (ICSID)

John Maynard Keynes (right) represented the UK at the conference, and Harry Dexter White represented the US.

The _____ is one of two major financial institutions created as a result of the Bretton Woods Conference in 1944. The International Monetary Fund, a related but separate institution, is the second.

   a. World Bank
   b. Bank-State-Branch
   c. Flow to Equity-Approach
   d. Financial costs of the 2003 Iraq War

19. _____, in microeconomics, are the cost advantages that a business obtains due to expansion. They are factors that cause a producere;s average cost per unit to fall as scale is increased. _____ is a long run concept and refers to reductions in unit cost as the size of a facility, or scale, increases.

   a. Underinvestment employment relationship
   b. Economic production quantity
   c. Economies of scale
   d. Isoquant

20. The phrase _____, according to the Organization for Economic Co-operation and Development, refers to 'creative work undertaken on a systematic basis in order to increase the stock of knowledge, including knowledge of man, culture and society, and the use of this stock of knowledge to devise new applications [sic]'

New product design and development is more than often a crucial factor in the survival of a company. In an industry that is fast changing, firms must continually revise their design and range of products. This is necessary due to continuous technology change and development as well as other competitors and the changing preference of customers.

   a. 100-year flood
   b. 130-30 fund
   c. 1921 recession
   d. Research and development

21. The _____ is a trilateral trade bloc in North America created by the governments of the United States, Canada, and Mexico. The agreement creating the trade bloc came into force on January 1, 1994. It superseded the Canada-United States Free Trade Agreement between the U.S. and Canada.

   a. Case-Shiller Home Price Indices
   b. Federal Reserve Bank Notes
   c. Demand-side technologies
   d. North American Free Trade Agreement

22. _____ is a type of trade policy that allows traders to act and transact without interference from government. Thus, the policy permits trading partners mutual gains from trade, with goods and services produced according to the theory of comparative advantage.

Under a _____ policy, prices are a reflection of true supply and demand, and are the sole determinant of resource allocation.

   a. 130-30 fund
   b. 100-year flood
   c. 1921 recession
   d. Free Trade

23. A _____ is the investment in a manufacturing, office, or other physical company-related structure or group of structures in an area where no previous facilities exist. The name comes from the idea of building a facility literally on a 'green' field, such as farmland or a forest. Over time the term has become more metaphoric.

a. Laddering
b. Greenfield investment
c. Master-feeder
d. Harbert Management Corporation

24. A _____ is an entity formed between two or more parties to undertake economic activity together. The parties agree to create a new entity by both contributing equity, and they then share in the revenues, expenses, and control of the enterprise. The venture can be for one specific project only, or a continuing business relationship such as the Fuji Xerox _____.
 a. Business valuation
 b. Nexus of contracts
 c. Property right
 d. Joint venture

25. An _____ is a person who has possession of an enterprise and assumes significant accountability for the inherent risks and the outcome. It is an ambitious leader who combines land, labor, and capital to create and market new goods or services. The term is a loanword from French and was first defined by the Irish economist Richard Cantillon.
 a. Entrepreneur
 b. ACCRA Cost of Living Index
 c. Expansionary policies
 d. ACEA agreement

Chapter 11. `Chips With Everything`: The Semiconductor Industry

1. In economics, an _____ is any good or commodity, transported from one country to another country in a legitimate fashion, typically for use in trade. _____ goods or services are provided to foreign consumers by domestic producers. _____ is an important part of international trade.
   a. ACCRA Cost of Living Index
   b. Export
   c. AD-IA Model
   d. ACEA agreement

2. In microeconomics, _____ is quite simply the conversion of inputs into outputs. It is an economic process that uses resources to create a good or service that is suitable for exchange. This can include manufacturing, storing, shipping, and packaging.
   a. MET
   b. Red Guards
   c. Solved
   d. Production

3. _____ is a comparative concept of the ability and performance of a firm, sub-sector or country to sell and supply goods and/or services in a given market. Although widely used in economics and business management, the usefulness of the concept, particularly in the context of national _____, is vigorously disputed by economists, such as Paul Krugman .

   The term may also be applied to markets, where it is used to refer to the extent to which the market structure may be regarded as perfectly competitive.

   a. Competitiveness
   b. Countervailing duties
   c. Debt moratorium
   d. Quota share

4. Economics:

   - _____, the desire to own something and the ability to pay for it
   - _____ curve, a graphic representation of a _____ schedule
   - _____ deposit, the money in checking accounts
   - _____ pull theory, the theory that inflation occurs when _____ for goods and services exceeds existing supplies
   - _____ schedule, a table that lists the quantity of a good a person will buy it each different price
   - _____ side economics, the school of economics at believes government spending and tax cuts open economy by raising _____

   a. Variability
   b. Demand
   c. Production
   d. McKesson ' Robbins scandal

5. _____ is a measure of the strength of a brand, product, service relative to competitive offerings. There is often a geographic element to the competitive landscape. In defining _____, you must see to what extent a product, brand, or firm controls a product category in a given geographic area.
   a. Demand shaping
   b. Market dominance
   c. Price elasticity of supply
   d. Horizontal territorial allocation

6. _____ in economics and business is the result of an exchange and from that trade we assign a numerical monetary value to a good, service or asset. If Alice trades Bob 4 apples for an orange, the _____ of an orange is 4 apples. Inversely, the _____ of an apple is 1/4 oranges.

| a. Price | b. Premium pricing |
| c. Price book | d. Price war |

7. _____ is any long-term change in the patterns of average weather of a specific region or the Earth as a whole. _____ reflects abnormal variations to the Earth's climate and subsequent effects on other parts of the Earth, such as in the ice caps over durations ranging from decades to millions of years.

In recent usage, especially in the context of environmental policy, _____ usually refers to changes in modern climate

| a. Climate Change | b. 1921 recession |
| c. 130-30 fund | d. 100-year flood |

8. The _____ is a protocol to the United Nations Framework Convention on Climate Change (UNFCCC or FCCC), an international environmental treaty produced at the United Nations Conference on treaty is intended to achieve 'stabilization of greenhouse gas concentrations in the atmosphere at a level that would prevent dangerous anthropogenic interference with the climate system.' The _____ establishes legally binding commitments for the reduction of four greenhouse gases (carbon dioxide, methane, nitrous oxide, sulphur hexafluoride), and two groups of gases (hydrofluorocarbons and perfluorocarbons) produced by 'Annex I' (industrialized) nations, as well as general commitments for all member countries. As of January 14 2009, 183 parties have ratified the protocol, which was initially adopted for use on 11 December 1997 in Kyoto, Japan and which entered into force on 16 February 2005. Under Kyoto, industrialized countries agreed to reduce their collective GHG emissions by 5.2% compared to the year 1990.

| a. Carbon offset | b. Greenhouse gases |
| c. Green New Deal | d. Kyoto Protocol |

9. _____ has several particular meanings:

- in mathematics
    - _____ function
    - Euler _____
    - _____
    - _____ subgroup
    - method of _____s (partial differential equations)
- in physics and engineering
    - any _____ curve that shows the relationship between certain input- and output parameters, e.g.
    - an I-V or current-voltage _____ is the current in a circuit as a function of the applied voltage
    - Receiver-Operator _____
- in fiction
    - in Dungeons ' Dragons, _____ is another name for ability score

| a. Russian financial crisis | b. Demand |
| c. Characteristic | d. Technocracy |

Chapter 11. `Chips With Everything`: The Semiconductor Industry

10. _____ or specialization is the specialization of cooperative labour in specific, circumscribed tasks and roles, intended to increase the productivity of labour. Historically the growth of a more and more complex _____ is closely associated with the growth of total output and trade, the rise of capitalism, and of the complexity of industrialization processes. Later, the _____ reached the level of a scientifically-based management practice with the time and motion studies associated with Taylorism.

   a. Day labor
   c. Work-life balance
   b. Demarcation dispute
   d. Division of labour

11. _____ is a cross-disciplinary area concerned with protecting the safety, health and welfare of people engaged in work or employment. As a secondary effect, it may also protect co-workers, family members, employers, customers, suppliers, nearby communities, and other members of the public who are impacted by the workplace environment. It may involve interactions among many subject areas, including occupational medicine, occupational (or industrial) hygiene, public health, safety engineering, chemistry, health physics, ergonomics, toxicology, epidemiology, environmental health, industrial relations, public policy, sociology, and occupational health psychology.

   a. Occupational safety and health
   c. AD-IA Model
   b. ACCRA Cost of Living Index
   d. ACEA agreement

12. _____ refers to the movement of cash into or out of a business or financial product. It is usually measured during a specified, finite period of time. Measurement of _____ can be used

- to determine a project's rate of return or value. The time of _____s into and out of projects are used as inputs in financial models such as internal rate of return, and net present value.
- to determine problems with a business's liquidity. Being profitable does not necessarily mean being liquid. A company can fail because of a shortage of cash, even while profitable.
- as an alternate measure of a business's profits when it is believed that accrual accounting concepts do not represent economic realities. For example, a company may be notionally profitable but generating little operational cash (as may be the case for a company that barters its products rather than selling for cash.) In such a case, the company may be deriving additional operating cash by issuing shares evaluating default risk, re-investment requirements, etc.

_____ is a generic term used differently depending on the context. It may be defined by users for their own purposes.

   a. Cash flow
   c. Restricted stock
   b. Second lien loan
   d. Strip financing

13. _____ is the economic policy of restraining trade between states, through methods such as tariffs on imported goods, restrictive quotas, and a variety of other restrictive government regulations designed to discourage imports, and prevent foreign take-over of local markets and companies. This policy is closely aligned with anti-globalization, and contrasts with free trade, where government barriers to trade are kept to a minimum. The term is mostly used in the context of economics, where _____ refers to policies or doctrines which 'protect' businesses and workers within a country by restricting or regulating trade with foreign nations.

   a. Knowledge economy
   c. Google economy
   b. Protectionism
   d. Digital economy

14. The _____ consists of a number of economic theories which describe the nature of the firm, company including its existence, its behaviour, and its relationship with the market.

In simplified terms, the _____ aims to answer these questions:

1. Existence - why do firms emerge, why are not all transactions in the economy mediated over the market?
2. Boundaries - why the boundary between firms and the market is located exactly there? Which transactions are performed internally and which are negotiated on the market?
3. Organization - why are firms structured in such specific way? What is the interplay of formal and informal relationships?

Despite looking simple, these questions are not answered by the established economic theory, which usually views firms as given, and treats them as black boxes without any internal structure.

The First World War period saw a change of emphasis in economic theory away from industry-level analysis which mainly included analysing markets to analysis at the level of the firm, as it became increasingly clear that perfect competition was no longer an adequate model of how firms behaved. Economic theory till then had focussed on trying to understand markets alone and there had been little study on understanding why firms or organisations exist.

    a. Khazzoom-Brookes postulate   b. Policy Ineffectiveness Proposition
    c. Technology gap   d. Theory of the firm

15. In finance, _____ is investment originating from other countries. See Foreign direct investment.
    a. Preclusive purchasing   b. Horizontal merger
    c. Demand side economics   d. Foreign investment

16. A _____ is an entity formed between two or more parties to undertake economic activity together. The parties agree to create a new entity by both contributing equity, and they then share in the revenues, expenses, and control of the enterprise. The venture can be for one specific project only, or a continuing business relationship such as the Fuji Xerox _____.
    a. Business valuation   b. Property right
    c. Nexus of contracts   d. Joint venture

17. An _____ is a person who has possession of an enterprise and assumes significant accountability for the inherent risks and the outcome. It is an ambitious leader who combines land, labor, and capital to create and market new goods or services. The term is a loanword from French and was first defined by the Irish economist Richard Cantillon.
    a. Entrepreneur   b. Expansionary policies
    c. ACCRA Cost of Living Index   d. ACEA agreement

18. _____ is a forum for 21 Pacific Rim countries (styled 'member economies') to cooperate on regional trade and investment liberalisation and facilitation. APEC's objective is to enhance economic growth and prosperity in the region and to strengthen the Asia-Pacific community. Members account for approximately 40% of the world's population, approximately 54% of world GDP and about 44% of world trade.
    a. AD-IA Model   b. Asia-Pacific Economic Cooperation
    c. ACCRA Cost of Living Index   d. ACEA agreement

19. The _____ is an economic and political union of 27 member states, located primarily in Europe. It was established by the Treaty of Maastricht on 1 November 1993, upon the foundations of the pre-existing European Economic Community. With a population of almost 500 million, the _____ generates an estimated 30% share (US$18.4 trillion in 2008) of the nominal gross world product.
   a. ACCRA Cost of Living Index
   b. European Court of Justice
   c. ACEA agreement
   d. European Union

20. The _____ is a trilateral trade bloc in North America created by the governments of the United States, Canada, and Mexico. The agreement creating the trade bloc came into force on January 1, 1994. It superseded the Canada-United States Free Trade Agreement between the U.S. and Canada.
   a. Case-Shiller Home Price Indices
   b. Federal Reserve Bank Notes
   c. North American Free Trade Agreement
   d. Demand-side technologies

Chapter 12. `Making the World Go Round`: The Financial Services Industries

1. _____ refer to services provided by the finance industry. The finance industry encompasses a broad range of organizations that deal with the management of money. Among these organizations are banks, credit card companies, insurance companies, consumer finance companies, stock brokerages, investment funds and some government sponsored enterprises.
   - a. Virtual Bidding
   - b. Minimum acceptable rate of return
   - c. Delta neutral
   - d. Financial services

2. _____ is a type of trade policy that allows traders to act and transact without interference from government. Thus, the policy permits trading partners mutual gains from trade, with goods and services produced according to the theory of comparative advantage.

   Under a _____ policy, prices are a reflection of true supply and demand, and are the sole determinant of resource allocation.
   - a. 1921 recession
   - b. Free Trade
   - c. 100-year flood
   - d. 130-30 fund

3. _____ is an economic system in which wealth, and the means of producing wealth, are privately owned. Through _____, the land, labor, and capital are owned, operated, and traded for the purpose of generating profits, without force or fraud, by private individuals either singly or jointly, and investments, distribution, income, production, pricing and supply of goods, commodities and services are determined by voluntary private decision in a market economy. A distinguishing feature of _____ is that each person owns his or her own labor and therefore is allowed to sell the use of it to employers.
   - a. Creative capitalism
   - b. Late capitalism
   - c. Socialism for the rich and capitalism for the poor
   - d. Capitalism

4. _____ is money accepted for exchange of goods in an economy. The prevalence of one money over another arises, usually, when a government designates through decrees that the government shall accept only particular notes and coins in payment for taxes. Typically, money of _____ consists of stamped coins and minted paper bills.
   - a. Local currency
   - b. Currency
   - c. Totnes pound
   - d. Security thread

5. In finance, the _____s between two currencies specifies how much one currency is worth in terms of the other. It is the value of a foreign natione;s currency in terms of the home natione;s currency. For example an _____ of 102 Japanese yen to the United States dollar means that JPY 102 is worth the same as USD 1.
   - a. ACEA agreement
   - b. ACCRA Cost of Living Index
   - c. Exchange rate
   - d. Interbank market

6. The term financial crisis is applied broadly to a variety of situations in which some financial institutions or assets suddenly lose a large part of their value. In the 19th and early 20th centuries, many _____ were associated with banking panics, and many recessions coincided with these panics. Other situations that are often called _____ include stock market crashes and the bursting of other financial bubbles, currency crises, and sovereign defaults.
   - a. Financial crises
   - b. Microeconomics
   - c. Georgism
   - d. General equilibrium

7. _____s is the social science that studies the production, distribution, and consumption of goods and services. The term _____s comes from the Ancient Greek oá¼°κονομῖα from oá¼¶κος (oikos, 'house') + vÏŒμος (nomos, 'custom' or 'law'), hence 'rules of the house(hold)'. Current _____ models developed out of the broader field of political economy in the late 19th century, owing to a desire to use an empirical approach more akin to the physical sciences.
   a. Opportunity cost   b. Energy economics
   c. Inflation   d. Economic

8. A _____, reserve bank, or monetary authority is the entity responsible for the monetary policy of a country or of a group of member states. It is a bank that can lend money to other banks in times of need. Its primary responsibility is to maintain the stability of the national currency and money supply, but more active duties include controlling subsidized-loan interest rates, and acting as a lender of last resort to the banking sector during times of financial crisis (private banks often being integral to the national financial system.)
   a. 100-year flood   b. Central bank
   c. 1921 recession   d. 130-30 fund

9. A _____ refers to any type debt instrument, such as a loan, bond, mortgage that does not have a fixed rate of interest over the life of the instrument. Such debt typically uses an index or other base rate for establishing the interest rate for each relevant period. One of the most common rates to use as the basis for applying interest rates is the London Inter-bank Offered Rate, or LIBOR
   a. Floating interest rate   b. Disposal tax effect
   c. Moneylender   d. Money market

10. The term _____ is applied broadly to a variety of situations in which some financial institutions or assets suddenly lose a large part of their value. In the 19th and early 20th centuries, many financial crises were associated with banking panics, and many recessions coincided with these panics. Other situations that are often called financial crises include stock market crashes and the bursting of other financial bubbles, currency crises, and sovereign defaults.
   a. Macroeconomics   b. Co-operative economics
   c. Market failure   d. Financial crisis

11. _____ is a structured finance process that involves pooling and repackaging of cash-flow-producing financial assets into securities, which are then sold to investors. The term '_____' is derived from the fact that the form of financial instruments used to obtain funds from the investors are securities. As a portfolio risk backed by amortizing cash flows - and unlike general corporate debt - the credit quality of securitized debt is non-stationary due to changes in volatility that are time- and structure-dependent.
   a. BIfFI   b. Pattern day trader
   c. Dow Jones Indexes   d. Securitization

12. _____ or accounting is the art of communicating financial information about a business entity to users such as shareholders and managers. The communication is generally in the form of financial statements that show in money terms that show the economic resources under the control of management.

Such financial information is primarily used by lenders, managers, investors, tax authorities, and other decision makers to make resource allocation decisions between and within companies, organizations, and public agencies.

a. Accountancy
b. AD-IA Model
c. ACEA agreement
d. ACCRA Cost of Living Index

13.

A _____ is a type of financial intermediary and a type of bank. Commercial banking is also known as business banking. It is a bank that provides checking accounts, savings accounts, and money market accounts and that accepts time deposits.

a. Daylight overdraft
b. Lombard banking
c. Commercial bank
d. Bought deal

14. Economics:

- _____,the desire to own something and the ability to pay for it
- _____ curve,a graphic representation of a _____ schedule
- _____ deposit, the money in checking accounts
- _____ pull theory,the theory that inflation occurs when _____ for goods and services exceeds existing supplies
- _____ schedule,a table that lists the quantity of a good a person will buy it each different price
- _____ side economics,the school of economics at believes government spending and tax cuts open economy by raising _____

a. Production
b. Demand
c. Variability
d. McKesson ' Robbins scandal

15. _____ is the removal or simplification of government rules and regulations that constrain the operation of market forces. _____ does not mean elimination of laws against fraud, but eliminating or reducing government control of how business is done, thereby moving toward a more free market.

The stated rationale for '_____' is often that fewer and simpler regulations will lead to a raised level of competitiveness, therefore higher productivity, more efficiency and lower prices overall.

a. Macroeconomic policy instruments
b. Secular basis
c. Fundamental psychological law
d. Deregulation

16. In economics, _____ is the removal of intermediaries in a supply chain: 'cutting out the middleman'. Instead of going through traditional distribution channels, which had some type of intermediate (such as a distributor, wholesaler, broker, or agent), companies may now deal with every customer directly, for example via the Internet. One important factor is a drop in the cost of servicing customers directly.

a. Disintermediation
b. Business-to-government
c. Consumer-to-consumer
d. Cluetrain Manifesto

Chapter 12. `Making the World Go Round`: The Financial Services Industries

17. In economics, an _____ is any good or commodity, transported from one country to another country in a legitimate fashion, typically for use in trade. _____ goods or services are provided to foreign consumers by domestic producers. _____ is an important part of international trade.
   a. AD-IA Model
   b. Export
   c. ACEA agreement
   d. ACCRA Cost of Living Index

18. In economics, a _____ is a mechanism that allows people to easily buy and sell (trade) financial securities (such as stocks and bonds), commodities (such as precious metals or agricultural goods), and other fungible items of value at low transaction costs and at prices that reflect the efficient-market hypothesis.

   _____s have evolved significantly over several hundred years and are undergoing constant innovation to improve liquidity.

   Both general markets (where many commodities are traded) and specialized markets (where only one commodity is traded) exist.

   a. Convertible arbitrage
   b. Noise trader
   c. Market anomaly
   d. Financial market

19. _____, in law and economics, is a form of risk management primarily used to hedge against the risk of a contingent loss. _____ is defined as the equitable transfer of the risk of a loss, from one entity to another, in exchange for a premium, and can be thought of as a guaranteed small loss to prevent a large, possibly devastating loss. An insurer is a company selling the _____; an insured or policyholder is the person or entity buying the _____.
   a. ACCRA Cost of Living Index
   b. ACEA agreement
   c. AD-IA Model
   d. Insurance

20. _____ has been viewed as a process of increasing involvement of enterprises in international markets, although there is no agreed definition of _____ or international entrepreneurship. There are several _____ theories which try to explain why there are international activities.

   Adam Smith claimed that a country should specialise in, and export, commodities in which it had an absolute advantage.

   a. Unified growth theory
   b. Internationalization
   c. Uppsala model
   d. Economic problem

21. In United States banking, _____ is a marketing term for certain services offered primarily to larger business customers. It may be used to describe all bank accounts (such as checking accounts) provided to businesses of a certain size, but it is more often used to describe specific services such as cash concentration, zero balance accounting, and automated clearing house facilities. Sometimes, private banking customers are given _____ services.
   a. Customer Demand Planning
   b. Global tactical asset allocation
   c. Ten bagger
   d. Cash management

Chapter 12. `Making the World Go Round`: The Financial Services Industries

22. A _____ is a foreign exchange agreement between two parties to exchange principal and fixed rate interest payments on a loan in one currency for principal and fixed rate interest payments on an equal (regarding net present value) loan in another currency. _____s are motivated by comparative advantage. _____s were introduced by the World Bank in 1981 to obtain Swiss franks and German marks by exchanging cash flows with IBM.
   a. Foreign exchange spot trading
   b. Strong dollar policy
   c. Currency swap
   d. Non-deliverable forward

23. _____s are financial contracts whose values are derived from the value of something else (known as the underlying.) The underlying value on which a _____ is based can be an asset (e.g., commodities, equities (stocks), residential mortgages, commercial real estate, loans, bonds), an index (e.g., interest rates, exchange rates, stock market indices, consumer price index (CPI) -- see inflation _____s), weather conditions bonds or other forms of credit.
   a. 100-year flood
   b. Derivative
   c. 130-30 fund
   d. Second derivative

24. The _____ are the financial markets for derivatives. The market can be divided into two, that for exchange traded derivatives and that for over-the-counter derivatives. The legal nature of these products is very different as well as the way they are traded, though many market participants are active in both.
   a. Notional amount
   b. Local volatility
   c. Derivatives markets
   d. Dual currency deposit

25. _____ is a fee paid on borrowed assets. It is the price paid for the use of borrowed money , or, money earned by deposited funds . Assets that are sometimes lent with _____ include money, shares, consumer goods through hire purchase, major assets such as aircraft, and even entire factories in finance lease arrangements.
   a. Internal debt
   b. Insolvency
   c. Interest
   d. Asset protection

26. An _____ is the price a borrower pays for the use of money they do not own, for instance a small company might borrow from a bank to kick start their business, and the return a lender receives for deferring the use of funds, by lending it to the borrower. _____s are normally expressed as a percentage rate over the period of one year.

   _____s targets are also a vital tool of monetary policy and are used to control variables like investment, inflation, and unemployment.

   a. Enterprise value
   b. Interest rate
   c. Arrow-Debreu model
   d. ACCRA Cost of Living Index

27. _____ is a forum for 21 Pacific Rim countries (styled 'member economies') to cooperate on regional trade and investment liberalisation and facilitation. APEC's objective is to enhance economic growth and prosperity in the region and to strengthen the Asia-Pacific community. Members account for approximately 40% of the world's population, approximately 54% of world GDP and about 44% of world trade.
   a. ACEA agreement
   b. AD-IA Model
   c. ACCRA Cost of Living Index
   d. Asia-Pacific Economic Cooperation

Chapter 12. `Making the World Go Round`: The Financial Services Industries

28. The _____ is an economic and political union of 27 member states, located primarily in Europe. It was established by the Treaty of Maastricht on 1 November 1993, upon the foundations of the pre-existing European Economic Community. With a population of almost 500 million, the _____ generates an estimated 30% share (US$18.4 trillion in 2008) of the nominal gross world product.
   a. European Union
   b. ACCRA Cost of Living Index
   c. European Court of Justice
   d. ACEA agreement

29. The _____ is an international organization that oversees the global financial system by following the macroeconomic policies of its member countries, in particular those with an impact on exchange rates and the balance of payments. It is an organization formed to stabilize international exchange rates and facilitate development. It also offers financial and technical assistance to its members, making it an international lender of last resort.
   a. ACCRA Cost of Living Index
   b. Office of Thrift Supervision
   c. International Monetary Fund
   d. ACEA agreement

30. The _____ is a trilateral trade bloc in North America created by the governments of the United States, Canada, and Mexico. The agreement creating the trade bloc came into force on January 1, 1994. It superseded the Canada-United States Free Trade Agreement between the U.S. and Canada.
   a. North American Free Trade Agreement
   b. Case-Shiller Home Price Indices
   c. Federal Reserve Bank Notes
   d. Demand-side technologies

31. _____ is sometimes referred to as _____, actually it means Economic Monetary Union.

First ideas of an economic and monetary union in Europe were raised well before establishing the European Communities. For example, already in the League of Nations, Gustav Stresemann asked in 1929 for a European currency (Link) against the background of an increased economic division due to a number of new nation states in Europe after WWI.

   a. European Monetary Union
   b. Euro Interbank Offered Rate
   c. Exchange rate mechanism
   d. European Monetary System

32. An economic and _____ is a single market with a common currency. It is to be distinguished from a mere currency union, which does not involve a single market. This is the fifth stage of economic integration.
   a. Monetary Union
   b. Commercial invoice
   c. Free trade zone
   d. Customs union

33. The _____ is an important selective, mainly private, international organization designed by its founders to supervise and liberalize international trade. The organization officially commenced on 1 January 1995, under the Marrakesh Agreement, succeeding the 1947 General Agreement on Tariffs and Trade (GATT.)

The _____ deals with regulation of trade between participating countries; it provides a framework for negotiating and formalising trade agreements, and a dispute resolution process aimed at enforcing participants' adherence to _____ agreements which are signed by representatives of member governments and ratified by their parliaments.

a. Backus-Kehoe-Kydland consumption correlation puzzle	b. 2009 G-20 London summit protests
c. World Trade Organization	d. Bio-energy village

34. _____ is a Regional Trade Agreement among Argentina, Brazil, Paraguay and Uruguay founded in 1991 by the Treaty of Asunci>ón, which was later amended and updated by the 1994 Treaty of Ouro Preto. Its purpose is to promote free trade and the fluid movement of goods, people, and currency.

_____ origins trace back to 1985 when Presidents Ra>úl Alfons>ín of Argentina and Jos>é Sarney of Brazil signed the Argentina-Brazil Integration and Economics Cooperation Program or PICE .

a. 130-30 fund	b. 100-year flood
c. Free trade area	d. MERCOSUR

35. The phrase _____ and acquisitions refers to the aspect of corporate strategy, corporate finance and management dealing with the buying, selling and combining of different companies that can aid, finance, or help a growing company in a given industry grow rapidly without having to create another business entity.

An acquisition, also known as a takeover or a buyout, is the buying of one company (the 'target') by another. An acquisition may be friendly or hostile.

a. Mergers	b. Differential accumulation
c. Peace dividend	d. Political economy

36. A security is a fungible, negotiable instrument representing financial value. _____ are broadly categorized into debt _____; equity _____, e.g., common stocks; and derivative (finance) contracts such as forwards, futures, options and swaps. The company or other entity issuing the security is called the issuer.

a. Red herring prospectus	b. Pass-Through Certificates
c. Settlement risk	d. Securities

37. Economic interventionism or _____ is an action in a Market economy taken by a government, beyond the basic regulation of fraud and enforcement of contracts, in an effort to affect its own economy. Economic intervention can be aimed at a variety of political or economic objectives, such as promoting economic growth, increasing employment, raising wages, raising or reducing prices, promoting equality, managing the money supply and interest rates, increasing profits, or addressing market failures. The intervention may to direct, or indirect as in the case of indicative planning.

a. ACCRA Cost of Living Index	b. ACEA agreement
c. Economic Planning	d. AD-IA Model

Chapter 12. `Making the World Go Round`: The Financial Services Industries

38. _____ has several particular meanings:

- in mathematics
    - _____ function
    - Euler _____
    - _____
    - _____ subgroup
    - method of _____ s (partial differential equations)
- in physics and engineering
    - any _____ curve that shows the relationship between certain input- and output parameters, e.g.
    - an I-V or current-voltage _____ is the current in a circuit as a function of the applied voltage
    - Receiver-Operator _____
- in fiction
    - in Dungeons ' Dragons, _____ is another name for ability score

a. Russian financial crisis b. Technocracy
c. Characteristic d. Demand

39. _____ is the increase in the amount of the goods and services produced by an economy over time. It is conventionally measured as the percent rate of increase in real gross domestic product, or real GDP. Growth is usually calculated in real terms, i.e. inflation-adjusted terms, in order to net out the effect of inflation on the price of the goods and services produced.

a. AD-IA Model b. ACCRA Cost of Living Index
c. ACEA agreement d. Economic growth

40. The _____ is one of the world's most important central banks, responsible for monetary policy covering the 16 member States of the Eurozone. It was established by the European Union (EU) in 1998 with its headquarters in Frankfurt, Germany.

The predecessor to the _____ was the European Monetary Institute .

a. ACCRA Cost of Living Index b. ACEA agreement
c. AD-IA Model d. European Central Bank

41. An _____, although not precisely defined, is usually a low-tax, lightly regulated jurisdiction which specializes in providing the corporate and commercial infrastructure to facilitate the use of that jurisdiction for the formation of offshore companies and for the investment of offshore funds.

The term _____ is a relatively modern neologism, first coined in the 1980s. Although the terms are not synonymous, many leading offshore finance centres are regarded as 'tax havens', and the lack of precise definitions often leads to confusion between the concepts.

a. Asset-based loan b. Amortizing loan
c. Offshore financial centre d. Earnings growth

Chapter 13. `Making the Connections, Selling the Goods`: The Distribution Industries

1. In economics, an _____ is any good or commodity, transported from one country to another country in a legitimate fashion, typically for use in trade. _____ goods or services are provided to foreign consumers by domestic producers. _____ is an important part of international trade.
   - a. ACEA agreement
   - b. AD-IA Model
   - c. ACCRA Cost of Living Index
   - d. Export

2. _____ involves the 'matching' of lenders with savings to borrowers who need money by an agent or third party, such as a bank.

If this matching is successful, the lender obtains a positive rate of return, the borrower receives a return for risk taking and entrepeneurship and the banker receives a marginal return for making the successful match. If the borrower's speculative play with the depositor's funds does not pay off, the depositor can lose the savings borrowed by the borrower and the bank can face significant losses on its loan portfolio.
   - a. Arranger
   - b. Origination fee
   - c. Annual percentage rate
   - d. Intermediation

3. In microeconomics, _____ is quite simply the conversion of inputs into outputs. It is an economic process that uses resources to create a good or service that is suitable for exchange. This can include manufacturing, storing, shipping, and packaging.
   - a. Solved
   - b. MET
   - c. Red Guards
   - d. Production

4. A _____ or labor union is an organization of workers who have banded together to achieve common goals in key areas and working conditions. The _____, through its leadership, bargains with the employer on behalf of union members (rank and file members) and negotiates labor contracts (Collective bargaining) with employers. This may include the negotiation of wages, work rules, complaint procedures, rules governing hiring, firing and promotion of workers, benefits, workplace safety and policies.
   - a. Case-Shiller Home Price Indices
   - b. Guaranteed investment contracts
   - c. Trade union
   - d. Consumer goods

5. An _____ is a retailer that primarily uses the Internet as a medium for customers to shop for the goods or services provided.

The word _____ is a portmanteau word derived from 'electronic' and 'retailer', in a similar way to 'e-mail'. The word has been in use since at least 1995.
   - a. Electronic Data Interchange
   - b. Electronic commerce
   - c. Automated Clearing House
   - d. E-tailer

6. _____ is a broad label that refers to any individuals or households that use goods and services generated within the economy. The concept of a _____ is used in different contexts, so that the usage and significance of the term may vary.

Typically when business people and economists talk of _____s they are talking about person as _____, an aggregated commodity item with little individuality other than that expressed in the buy/not-buy decision.

Chapter 13. `Making the Connections, Selling the Goods`: The Distribution Industries   83

a. 100-year flood
c. 130-30 fund
b. Consumer
d. 1921 recession

7. Economics:

- _____, the desire to own something and the ability to pay for it
- _____ curve, a graphic representation of a _____ schedule
- _____ deposit, the money in checking accounts
- _____ pull theory, the theory that inflation occurs when _____ for goods and services exceeds existing supplies
- _____ schedule, a table that lists the quantity of a good a person will buy it each different price
- _____ side economics, the school of economics at believes government spending and tax cuts open economy by raising _____

a. McKesson ' Robbins scandal
c. Variability
b. Production
d. Demand

8. _____ refers to the structured transmission of data between organizations by electronic means. It is used to transfer electronic documents from one computer system to another (ie) from one trading partner to another trading partner. It is more than mere E-mail; for instance, organizations might replace bills of lading and even checks with appropriate _____ messages.

a. Auction software
c. E-tailer
b. Electronic data interchange
d. Electronic commerce

9. _____s is the social science that studies the production, distribution, and consumption of goods and services. The term _____s comes from the Ancient Greek oá¼°κονομῖα from oá¼¶κος (oikos, 'house') + vÏŒμος (nomos, 'custom' or 'law'), hence 'rules of the house(hold)'. Current _____ models developed out of the broader field of political economy in the late 19th century, owing to a desire to use an empirical approach more akin to the physical sciences.

a. Opportunity cost
c. Energy economics
b. Inflation
d. Economic

10. _____ is a practice in logistics of unloading materials from an incoming semi-trailer truck or rail car and loading these materials directly into outbound trucks, trailers with little or no storage in between. This may be done to change type of conveyance, to sort material intended for different destinations or similar destination.

Cross-Dock operations were first pioneered in the US trucking industry in the 1930's, and have been in continuous use in LTL (less than truckload) operations ever since.

a. Business development
c. Long squeeze
b. Business process automation
d. Cross-docking

11. _____ describes commerce transactions between businesses, such as between a manufacturer and a wholesaler, or between a wholesaler and a retailer. Contrasting terms are business-to-consumer (B2C) and business-to-government (B2G.)

The volume of B2B transactions is much higher than the volume of B2C transactions.

   a. Business-to-business
   c. Market sector
   b. Customer relationship management
   d. Customer to customer

   12. _____ is a forum for 21 Pacific Rim countries (styled 'member economies') to cooperate on regional trade and investment liberalisation and facilitation. APEC's objective is to enhance economic growth and prosperity in the region and to strengthen the Asia-Pacific community. Members account for approximately 40% of the world's population, approximately 54% of world GDP and about 44% of world trade.
   a. ACCRA Cost of Living Index
   c. AD-IA Model
   b. ACEA agreement
   d. Asia-Pacific Economic Cooperation

   13. The _____ is an economic and political union of 27 member states, located primarily in Europe. It was established by the Treaty of Maastricht on 1 November 1993, upon the foundations of the pre-existing European Economic Community. With a population of almost 500 million, the _____ generates an estimated 30% share (US$18.4 trillion in 2008) of the nominal gross world product.
   a. European Court of Justice
   c. ACCRA Cost of Living Index
   b. ACEA agreement
   d. European Union

   14. The _____ is a trilateral trade bloc in North America created by the governments of the United States, Canada, and Mexico. The agreement creating the trade bloc came into force on January 1, 1994. It superseded the Canada-United States Free Trade Agreement between the U.S. and Canada.
   a. Case-Shiller Home Price Indices
   c. Federal Reserve Bank Notes
   b. Demand-side technologies
   d. North American Free Trade Agreement

   15. _____ is a type of trade policy that allows traders to act and transact without interference from government. Thus, the policy permits trading partners mutual gains from trade, with goods and services produced according to the theory of comparative advantage.

Under a _____ policy, prices are a reflection of true supply and demand, and are the sole determinant of resource allocation.

   a. 130-30 fund
   c. 1921 recession
   b. 100-year flood
   d. Free Trade

   16. _____ is the removal or simplification of government rules and regulations that constrain the operation of market forces. _____ does not mean elimination of laws against fraud, but eliminating or reducing government control of how business is done, thereby moving toward a more free market.

The stated rationale for '_____' is often that fewer and simpler regulations will lead to a raised level of competitiveness, therefore higher productivity, more efficiency and lower prices overall.

   a. Macroeconomic policy instruments
   c. Deregulation
   b. Secular basis
   d. Fundamental psychological law

17. _____ is the transport of goods or passengers between two points in the same country. Originally starting with shipping, _____ now also covers aviation, railways and road transport. _____ is 'trade or navigation in coastal waters, or, the exclusive right of a country to operate the air traffic within its territory.'

_____ is commonly used as part of the term '_____ rights,' the right of a company from one country to trade in another country.

a. Business operations
b. Business process reengineering
c. Cross-docking
d. Cabotage

18. A _____ is an object whose consumption increases the utility of the consumer, for which the quantity demanded exceeds the quantity supplied at zero price. _____s are usually modeled as having diminishing marginal utility. The first individual purchase has high utility; the second has less.

a. Composite good
b. Pie method
c. Good
d. Merit good

19. In economics, economic output is divided into physical goods and intangible services. Consumption of _____ is assumed to produce utility. It is often used when referring to a _____ Tax.

a. Composite good
b. Private good
c. Manufactured goods
d. Goods and services

20. In economics, an _____ is any good (e.g. a commodity) or service brought into one country from another country in a legitimate fashion, typically for use in trade. It is a good that is brought in from another country for sale. _____ goods or services are provided to domestic consumers by foreign producers. An _____ in the receiving country is an export to the sending country.

a. Incoterms
b. Import quota
c. Economic integration
d. Import

21. A _____ is a business that is privately owned and operated, with a small number of employees and relatively low volume of sales. The legal definition of 'small' often varies by country and industry, but is generally under 100 employees in the United States and under 50 employees in the European Union. In comparison, the definition of mid-sized business by the number of employees is generally under 500 in the U.S. and 250 for the European Union.

a. Small Business
b. Procurement
c. Cabotage
d. Farmshoring

22. A _____ is a set of companies with interlocking business relationships and shareholdings. It is a type of business group.

The prototypical _____ are those which appeared in Japan during the 'economic miracle' following World War II.

a. 1921 recession
b. 130-30 fund
c. 100-year flood
d. Keiretsu

23. The _____ consists of a number of economic theories which describe the nature of the firm, company including its existence, its behaviour, and its relationship with the market.

Chapter 13. `Making the Connections, Selling the Goods`: The Distribution Industries

In simplified terms, the _____ aims to answer these questions:

1. Existence - why do firms emerge, why are not all transactions in the economy mediated over the market?
2. Boundaries - why the boundary between firms and the market is located exactly there? Which transactions are performed internally and which are negotiated on the market?
3. Organization - why are firms structured in such specific way? What is the interplay of formal and informal relationships?

Despite looking simple, these questions are not answered by the established economic theory, which usually views firms as given, and treats them as black boxes without any internal structure.

The First World War period saw a change of emphasis in economic theory away from industry-level analysis which mainly included analysing markets to analysis at the level of the firm, as it became increasingly clear that perfect competition was no longer an adequate model of how firms behaved. Economic theory till then had focussed on trying to understand markets alone and there had been little study on understanding why firms or organisations exist.

a. Theory of the firm
b. Technology gap
c. Policy Ineffectiveness Proposition
d. Khazzoom-Brookes postulate

24. The phrase _____ and acquisitions refers to the aspect of corporate strategy, corporate finance and management dealing with the buying, selling and combining of different companies that can aid, finance, or help a growing company in a given industry grow rapidly without having to create another business entity.

An acquisition, also known as a takeover or a buyout, is the buying of one company (the 'target') by another. An acquisition may be friendly or hostile.

a. Differential accumulation
b. Political economy
c. Peace dividend
d. Mergers

25. A _____ is the subset of the market on which a specific product is focusing on; Therefore the market niche defines the specific product features aimed at satisfying specific market needs, as well as the price range, production quality and the demographics that is intending to impact.

Every single product that is on sale can be defined by its _____. As of special note, the products aimed at a wide demographics audience, with the resulting low price (due to Price elasticity of demand), are said to belong to the Mainstream niche, in practice referred only as Mainstream or of high demand.

a. Niche market
b. Celebrity-industrial complex
c. Market manipulation
d. Marginal efficiency of capital

Chapter 14. Winners and Losers: An Overview

1. _____s is the social science that studies the production, distribution, and consumption of goods and services. The term _____s comes from the Ancient Greek οἰκονομῖα from οἶκος (oikos, 'house') + νόμος (nomos, 'custom' or 'law'), hence 'rules of the house(hold)'. Current _____ models developed out of the broader field of political economy in the late 19th century, owing to a desire to use an empirical approach more akin to the physical sciences.
   a. Opportunity cost
   b. Energy economics
   c. Inflation
   d. Economic

2. The _____ consists of a number of economic theories which describe the nature of the firm, company including its existence, its behaviour, and its relationship with the market.

In simplified terms, the _____ aims to answer these questions:

   1. Existence - why do firms emerge, why are not all transactions in the economy mediated over the market?
   2. Boundaries - why the boundary between firms and the market is located exactly there? Which transactions are performed internally and which are negotiated on the market?
   3. Organization - why are firms structured in such specific way? What is the interplay of formal and informal relationships?

Despite looking simple, these questions are not answered by the established economic theory, which usually views firms as given, and treats them as black boxes without any internal structure.

The First World War period saw a change of emphasis in economic theory away from industry-level analysis which mainly included analysing markets to analysis at the level of the firm, as it became increasingly clear that perfect competition was no longer an adequate model of how firms behaved. Economic theory till then had focussed on trying to understand markets alone and there had been little study on understanding why firms or organisations exist.

   a. Theory of the firm
   b. Technology gap
   c. Policy Ineffectiveness Proposition
   d. Khazzoom-Brookes postulate

3. _____ is the removal or simplification of government rules and regulations that constrain the operation of market forces. _____ does not mean elimination of laws against fraud, but eliminating or reducing government control of how business is done, thereby moving toward a more free market.

The stated rationale for '_____' is often that fewer and simpler regulations will lead to a raised level of competitiveness, therefore higher productivity, more efficiency and lower prices overall.

   a. Macroeconomic policy instruments
   b. Fundamental psychological law
   c. Secular basis
   d. Deregulation

4. In economics, an _____ is any good or commodity, transported from one country to another country in a legitimate fashion, typically for use in trade. _____ goods or services are provided to foreign consumers by domestic producers. _____ is an important part of international trade.
   a. ACEA agreement
   b. AD-IA Model
   c. ACCRA Cost of Living Index
   d. Export

5. _____ is the shortage of common things such as food, clothing, shelter and safe drinking water, all of which determine the quality of life. It may also include the lack of access to opportunities such as education and employment which aid the escape from _____ and/or allow one to enjoy the respect of fellow citizens. According to Mollie Orshansky who developed the _____ measurements used by the U.S. government, 'to be poor is to be deprived of those goods and services and pleasures which others around us take for granted.' Ongoing debates over causes, effects and best ways to measure _____, directly influence the design and implementation of _____-reduction programs and are therefore relevant to the fields of public administration and international development.

   a. Poverty map   b. Liberal welfare reforms
   c. Growth Elasticity of Poverty   d. Poverty

6. In statistics, the _____ problem occurs when one considers a set of statistical inferences simultaneously. Errors in inference, including confidence intervals that fail to include their corresponding population parameters are more likely to occur when one considers the family as a whole. Several statistical techniques have been developed to prevent this from happening, allowing significance levels for single and _____ to be directly compared.

   a. Familywise error rate   b. False discovery rate
   c. Hypotheses suggested by the data   d. Multiple comparisons

7. _____ is defined as the number of deaths of infants (one year of age or younger) per 1000 live births. The most common cause of _____ worldwide has traditionally been dehydration from diarrhea. Because of the success of spreading information about Oral Rehydration Solution (a mixture of salts, sugar, and water) to mothers around the world, the rate of children dying from dehydration has been decreasing and has become the second most common cause in the late 1990s.

   a. ACCRA Cost of Living Index   b. AD-IA Model
   c. ACEA agreement   d. Infant mortality

8. _____ is a measure of the number of deaths (in general scaled to the size of that population, per unit time. _____ is typically expressed in units of deaths per 1000 individuals per year; thus, a _____ of 9.5 in a population of 100,000 would mean 950 deaths per year in that entire population. It is distinct from morbidity rate, which refers to the number of individuals in poor health during a given time period (the prevalence rate) or the number who currently have that disease (the incidence rate), scaled to the size of the population.

   a. Mortality rate   b. 1921 recession
   c. 100-year flood   d. 130-30 fund

9. _____ is the change in population over time, and can be quantified as the change in the number of individuals in a population using 'per unit time' for measurement. The term _____ can technically refer to any species, but almost always refers to humans, and it is often used informally for the more specific demographic term _____ rate , and is often used to refer specifically to the growth of the population of the world.

Simple models of _____ include the Malthusian Growth Model and the logistic model.

   a. Population growth   b. 100-year flood
   c. Population dynamics   d. 130-30 fund

10. _____ is a type of trade policy that allows traders to act and transact without interference from government. Thus, the policy permits trading partners mutual gains from trade, with goods and services produced according to the theory of comparative advantage.

Under a _____ policy, prices are a reflection of true supply and demand, and are the sole determinant of resource allocation.

a. Free Trade
c. 1921 recession
b. 130-30 fund
d. 100-year flood

11. In finance, _____ is investment originating from other countries. See Foreign direct investment.
a. Demand side economics
c. Horizontal merger
b. Preclusive purchasing
d. Foreign investment

12. _____ is any long-term change in the patterns of average weather of a specific region or the Earth as a whole. _____ reflects abnormal variations to the Earth's climate and subsequent effects on other parts of the Earth, such as in the ice caps over durations ranging from decades to millions of years.

In recent usage, especially in the context of environmental policy, _____ usually refers to changes in modern climate

a. 1921 recession
c. 100-year flood
b. 130-30 fund
d. Climate Change

13. The _____ is a protocol to the United Nations Framework Convention on Climate Change (UNFCCC or FCCC), an international environmental treaty produced at the United Nations Conference on treaty is intended to achieve 'stabilization of greenhouse gas concentrations in the atmosphere at a level that would prevent dangerous anthropogenic interference with the climate system.' The _____ establishes legally binding commitments for the reduction of four greenhouse gases (carbon dioxide, methane, nitrous oxide, sulphur hexafluoride), and two groups of gases (hydrofluorocarbons and perfluorocarbons) produced by 'Annex I' (industrialized) nations, as well as general commitments for all member countries. As of January 14 2009, 183 parties have ratified the protocol, which was initially adopted for use on 11 December 1997 in Kyoto, Japan and which entered into force on 16 February 2005. Under Kyoto, industrialized countries agreed to reduce their collective GHG emissions by 5.2% compared to the year 1990.

a. Green New Deal
c. Carbon offset
b. Greenhouse gases
d. Kyoto Protocol

Chapter 15. Making a Living in Developed Countries: Where Will the Jobs Come From?

1. In economics, an _____ is any good or commodity, transported from one country to another country in a legitimate fashion, typically for use in trade. _____ goods or services are provided to foreign consumers by domestic producers. _____ is an important part of international trade.
   a. AD-IA Model
   b. Export
   c. ACCRA Cost of Living Index
   d. ACEA agreement

2. _____ is any long-term change in the patterns of average weather of a specific region or the Earth as a whole. _____ reflects abnormal variations to the Earth's climate and subsequent effects on other parts of the Earth, such as in the ice caps over durations ranging from decades to millions of years.

   In recent usage, especially in the context of environmental policy, _____ usually refers to changes in modern climate

   a. Climate Change
   b. 100-year flood
   c. 130-30 fund
   d. 1921 recession

3. The _____ is a protocol to the United Nations Framework Convention on Climate Change (UNFCCC or FCCC), an international environmental treaty produced at the United Nations Conference on treaty is intended to achieve 'stabilization of greenhouse gas concentrations in the atmosphere at a level that would prevent dangerous anthropogenic interference with the climate system.' The _____ establishes legally binding commitments for the reduction of four greenhouse gases (carbon dioxide, methane, nitrous oxide, sulphur hexafluoride), and two groups of gases (hydrofluorocarbons and perfluorocarbons) produced by 'Annex I' (industrialized) nations, as well as general commitments for all member countries. As of January 14 2009, 183 parties have ratified the protocol, which was initially adopted for use on 11 December 1997 in Kyoto, Japan and which entered into force on 16 February 2005. Under Kyoto, industrialized countries agreed to reduce their collective GHG emissions by 5.2% compared to the year 1990.
   a. Green New Deal
   b. Greenhouse gases
   c. Carbon offset
   d. Kyoto Protocol

4. _____ is a specific term used in companies' financial reporting from the company-whole point of view. Because that use excludes the effects of changing ownership interest, an economic measure of _____ is necessary for financial analysis from the shareholders' point of view

   _____ is defined by the Financial Accounting Standards Board, or FASB, as e;the change in equity [net assets] of a business enterprise during a period from transactions and other events and circumstances from nonowner sources. It includes all changes in equity during a period except those resulting from investments by owners and distributions to owners.e;

   _____ is the sum of net income and other items that must bypass the income statement because they have not been realized, including items like an unrealized holding gain or loss from available for sale securities and foreign currency translation gains or losses.

   a. Windfall gain
   b. Real income
   c. Net national income
   d. Comprehensive income

5. In finance, _____ is investment originating from other countries.See Foreign direct investment.

Chapter 15. Making a Living in Developed Countries: Where Will the Jobs Come From?

a. Demand side economics
b. Foreign investment
c. Horizontal merger
d. Preclusive purchasing

6. _____ to the arrival of new individuals into a habitat or population. It is a biological concept and is important in population ecology, differentiated from emigration and migration.

_____ is a modern phenomenon.

a. AD-IA Model
b. ACEA agreement
c. ACCRA Cost of Living Index
d. Immigration

7. _____s is the social science that studies the production, distribution, and consumption of goods and services. The term _____s comes from the Ancient Greek οἰκονομία from οἶκος (oikos, 'house') + νόμος (nomos, 'custom' or 'law'), hence 'rules of the house(hold)'. Current _____ models developed out of the broader field of political economy in the late 19th century, owing to a desire to use an empirical approach more akin to the physical sciences.

a. Energy economics
b. Inflation
c. Economic
d. Opportunity cost

8. In mathematics, an _____ is a statement about the relative size or order of two objects, or about whether they are the same or not

- The notation a < b means that a is less than b.
- The notation a > b means that a is greater than b.
- The notation a ≠ b means that a is not equal to b, but does not say that one is greater than the other or even that they can be compared in size.

In each statement above, a is not equal to b. These relations are known as strict inequalities. The notation a < b may also be read as 'a is strictly less than b'.

a. ACEA agreement
b. ACCRA Cost of Living Index
c. AD-IA Model
d. Inequality

9. The process of _____ involves the introduction of a good or service that is new or substantially improved. This includes, but is not limited to, improvements in functional characteristics, technical abilities, or ease of use.

a. Product innovation
b. Refusal to deal
c. Dogs of the Dow
d. Microcap stock

10. In economics, a _____ is a general slowdown in economic activity over a sustained period of time, or a business cycle contraction. During _____s, many macroeconomic indicators vary in a similar way. Production as measured by Gross Domestic Product (GDP), employment, investment spending, capacity utilization, household incomes and business profits all fall during _____s.

a. Leading indicators
b. Monetary economics
c. Treasury View
d. Recession

Chapter 15. Making a Living in Developed Countries: Where Will the Jobs Come From?

11. _____ is a term that is used to describe the overall process of invention, innovation and diffusion of technology or processes. The term is redundant with technological development, technological achievement, and technological progress. In essence _____ is the invention of a technology (or a process), the continuous process of improving a technology (in which it often becomes cheaper) and its diffusion throughout industry or society.
   a. 130-30 fund
   b. 100-year flood
   c. 1921 recession
   d. Technological change

12. _____ in its literal sense is the process of transformation of local or regional phenomena into global ones. It can be described as a process by which the people of the world are unified into a single society and function together.

This process is a combination of economic, technological, sociocultural and political forces.

   a. Globalization
   b. Global Cosmopolitanism
   c. Helsinki Process on Globalisation and Democracy
   d. Globally Integrated Enterprise

13. A _____ is any worker who has some special skill, knowledge, or (usually acquired) ability in his work. A _____ may have attended a college, university or technical school. Or, a _____ may have learned his skills on the job.
   a. Time and attendance
   b. Timebar scheduling
   c. Global Career Development Facilitator
   d. Skilled worker

14. A _____ is a country that has low standards of democratic governments, industrialization, social programs, and human rights guarantees that are yet to develop to those met in the West. It is often a term used to describe a nation with a low level of material well being. Despite this definition, the levels of development may vary, with some developing countries having higher average standards of living.
   a. Technology governance
   b. Luddite fallacy
   c. Habakkuk thesis
   d. Developing country

15. In economics, an _____ is any good (e.g. a commodity) or service brought into one country from another country in a legitimate fashion, typically for use in trade. It is a good that is brought in from another country for sale. _____ goods or services are provided to domestic consumers by foreign producers. An _____ in the receiving country is an export to the sending country.
   a. Incoterms
   b. Import quota
   c. Economic integration
   d. Import

16. _____ is the increase in the amount of the goods and services produced by an economy over time. It is conventionally measured as the percent rate of increase in real gross domestic product, or real GDP. Growth is usually calculated in real terms, i.e. inflation-adjusted terms, in order to net out the effect of inflation on the price of the goods and services produced.
   a. ACCRA Cost of Living Index
   b. ACEA agreement
   c. AD-IA Model
   d. Economic growth

17. _____ is the removal or simplification of government rules and regulations that constrain the operation of market forces. _____ does not mean elimination of laws against fraud, but eliminating or reducing government control of how business is done, thereby moving toward a more free market.

Chapter 15. Making a Living in Developed Countries: Where Will the Jobs Come From?

The stated rationale for '_____' is often that fewer and simpler regulations will lead to a raised level of competitiveness, therefore higher productivity, more efficiency and lower prices overall.

a. Macroeconomic policy instruments
b. Deregulation
c. Secular basis
d. Fundamental psychological law

18. The phrase _____ and acquisitions refers to the aspect of corporate strategy, corporate finance and management dealing with the buying, selling and combining of different companies that can aid, finance, or help a growing company in a given industry grow rapidly without having to create another business entity.

An acquisition, also known as a takeover or a buyout, is the buying of one company (the 'target') by another. An acquisition may be friendly or hostile.

a. Political economy
b. Differential accumulation
c. Mergers
d. Peace dividend

19. _____ is the incidence or process of transferring ownership of a business, enterprise, agency or public service from the public sector (government) to the private sector (business.) In a broader sense, _____ refers to transfer of any government function to the private sector including governmental functions like revenue collection and law enforcement.

The term '_____' also has been used to describe two unrelated transactions.

a. Privatization
b. Compound empowerment
c. Ricardian equivalence
d. Performance reports

20. The _____ is an economic and political union of 27 member states, located primarily in Europe. It was established by the Treaty of Maastricht on 1 November 1993, upon the foundations of the pre-existing European Economic Community. With a population of almost 500 million, the _____ generates an estimated 30% share (US$18.4 trillion in 2008) of the nominal gross world product.

a. ACCRA Cost of Living Index
b. ACEA agreement
c. European Court of Justice
d. European Union

21. _____ according to Onuoha (2007) is the practice of starting new organizations or revitalizing mature organizations, particularly new businesses generally in response to identified opportunities. _____ is often a difficult undertaking, as a vast majority of new businesses fail. Entrepreneurial activities are substantially different depending on the type of organization that is being started.

a. Intrapreneurship
b. Entrepreneurship
c. ACEA agreement
d. ACCRA Cost of Living Index

22. _____ in its classic form is defined as a company from one country making a physical investment into building a factory in another country. It is the establishment of an enterprise by a foreigner. Its definition can be extended to include investments made to acquire lasting interest in enterprises operating outside of the economy of the investor.

a. Foreign direct investment
b. Federal Deposit Insurance Corporation
c. Financial Stability Forum
d. Non-governmental organization

94 *Chapter 15. Making a Living in Developed Countries: Where Will the Jobs Come From?*

23. _____ is an economic system in which wealth, and the means of producing wealth, are privately owned. Through _____, the land, labor, and capital are owned, operated, and traded for the purpose of generating profits, without force or fraud, by private individuals either singly or jointly, and investments, distribution, income, production, pricing and supply of goods, commodities and services are determined by voluntary private decision in a market economy. A distinguishing feature of _____ is that each person owns his or her own labor and therefore is allowed to sell the use of it to employers.
    a. Late capitalism
    b. Creative capitalism
    c. Socialism for the rich and capitalism for the poor
    d. Capitalism

24. _____ is the economic policy of restraining trade between states, through methods such as tariffs on imported goods, restrictive quotas, and a variety of other restrictive government regulations designed to discourage imports, and prevent foreign take-over of local markets and companies. This policy is closely aligned with anti-globalization, and contrasts with free trade, where government barriers to trade are kept to a minimum. The term is mostly used in the context of economics, where _____ refers to policies or doctrines which 'protect' businesses and workers within a country by restricting or regulating trade with foreign nations.
    a. Protectionism
    b. Google economy
    c. Knowledge economy
    d. Digital economy

25. _____ is a type of trade policy that allows traders to act and transact without interference from government. Thus, the policy permits trading partners mutual gains from trade, with goods and services produced according to the theory of comparative advantage.

Under a _____ policy, prices are a reflection of true supply and demand, and are the sole determinant of resource allocation.

   a. 100-year flood
   b. Free Trade
   c. 130-30 fund
   d. 1921 recession

Chapter 16. Making a Living in Developing Countries: Sustaining Growth, Enhancing Equity

1. _____ is defined as the number of deaths of infants (one year of age or younger) per 1000 live births. The most common cause of _____ worldwide has traditionally been dehydration from diarrhea. Because of the success of spreading information about Oral Rehydration Solution (a mixture of salts, sugar, and water) to mothers around the world, the rate of children dying from dehydration has been decreasing and has become the second most common cause in the late 1990s.
    a. ACCRA Cost of Living Index
    b. AD-IA Model
    c. Infant mortality
    d. ACEA agreement

2. _____ is a measure of the number of deaths (in general scaled to the size of that population, per unit time. _____ is typically expressed in units of deaths per 1000 individuals per year; thus, a _____ of 9.5 in a population of 100,000 would mean 950 deaths per year in that entire population. It is distinct from morbidity rate, which refers to the number of individuals in poor health during a given time period (the prevalence rate) or the number who currently have that disease (the incidence rate), scaled to the size of the population.
    a. 100-year flood
    b. 130-30 fund
    c. 1921 recession
    d. Mortality rate

3. _____ is a type of trade policy that allows traders to act and transact without interference from government. Thus, the policy permits trading partners mutual gains from trade, with goods and services produced according to the theory of comparative advantage.

Under a _____ policy, prices are a reflection of true supply and demand, and are the sole determinant of resource allocation.

    a. 1921 recession
    b. 100-year flood
    c. 130-30 fund
    d. Free Trade

4. In economics, an _____ is any good or commodity, transported from one country to another country in a legitimate fashion, typically for use in trade. _____ goods or services are provided to foreign consumers by domestic producers. _____ is an important part of international trade.
    a. Export
    b. ACCRA Cost of Living Index
    c. AD-IA Model
    d. ACEA agreement

5. _____ is any long-term change in the patterns of average weather of a specific region or the Earth as a whole. _____ reflects abnormal variations to the Earth's climate and subsequent effects on other parts of the Earth, such as in the ice caps over durations ranging from decades to millions of years.

In recent usage, especially in the context of environmental policy, _____ usually refers to changes in modern climate

    a. Climate Change
    b. 130-30 fund
    c. 1921 recession
    d. 100-year flood

96 *Chapter 16. Making a Living in Developing Countries: Sustaining Growth, Enhancing Equity*

6. The _____ is a protocol to the United Nations Framework Convention on Climate Change (UNFCCC or FCCC), an international environmental treaty produced at the United Nations Conference on treaty is intended to achieve 'stabilization of greenhouse gas concentrations in the atmosphere at a level that would prevent dangerous anthropogenic interference with the climate system.' The _____ establishes legally binding commitments for the reduction of four greenhouse gases (carbon dioxide, methane, nitrous oxide, sulphur hexafluoride), and two groups of gases (hydrofluorocarbons and perfluorocarbons) produced by 'Annex I' (industrialized) nations, as well as general commitments for all member countries. As of January 14 2009, 183 parties have ratified the protocol, which was initially adopted for use on 11 December 1997 in Kyoto, Japan and which entered into force on 16 February 2005. Under Kyoto, industrialized countries agreed to reduce their collective GHG emissions by 5.2% compared to the year 1990.

 a. Kyoto Protocol
 b. Carbon offset
 c. Green New Deal
 d. Greenhouse gases

7. In economics, _____ describes the state of a market with respect to competition.

- Perfect competition, in which the market consists of a very large number of firms producing a homogeneous product.
- Monopolistic competition where there are a large number of independent firms which have a very small proportion of the market share.
- Oligopoly, in which a market is dominated by a small number of firms which own more than 40% of the market share.
- Oligopsony, a market dominated by many sellers and a few buyers.
- Monopoly, where there is only one provider of a product or service.
- Natural monopoly, a monopoly in which economies of scale cause efficiency to increase continuously with the size of the firm. A firm is a natural monopoly if it is able to serve the entire market demand at a lower cost than any combination of two or more smaller, more specialized firms.
- Monopsony, when there is only one buyer in a market.

The imperfectly competitive structure is quite identical to the realistic market conditions where some monopolistic competitors, monopolists, oligopolists, and duopolists exist and dominate the market conditions. The elements of _____ include the number and size distribution of firms, entry conditions, and the extent of differentiation.

These somewhat abstract concerns tend to determine some but not all details of a specific concrete market system where buyers and sellers actually meet and commit to trade.

 a. Market structure
 b. Human capital
 c. Labour economics
 d. Monopolistic competition

8. In finance, _____ is investment originating from other countries. See Foreign direct investment.
 a. Preclusive purchasing
 b. Horizontal merger
 c. Demand side economics
 d. Foreign investment

9. _____ is the shortage of common things such as food, clothing, shelter and safe drinking water, all of which determine the quality of life. It may also include the lack of access to opportunities such as education and employment which aid the escape from _____ and/or allow one to enjoy the respect of fellow citizens. According to Mollie Orshansky who developed the _____ measurements used by the U.S. government, 'to be poor is to be deprived of those goods and services and pleasures which others around us take for granted.' Ongoing debates over causes, effects and best ways to measure _____, directly influence the design and implementation of _____-reduction programs and are therefore relevant to the fields of public administration and international development.

Chapter 16. Making a Living in Developing Countries: Sustaining Growth, Enhancing Equity   97

    a. Growth Elasticity of Poverty
    c. Liberal welfare reforms
    b. Poverty
    d. Poverty map

10. In economics, the term _____ has three different distinct meanings and applications. While it is related to unemployment, a situation in which a person who is searching for work cannot find a job, in the case of _____, a person is working. All three of the definitions of '_____' involve underutilization of labor that critics say is missed by most official (governmental agency) definitions and measurements of unemployment.
    a. Employability
    c. Underemployment
    b. Informational interview
    d. Encore career

11. _____s is the social science that studies the production, distribution, and consumption of goods and services. The term _____s comes from the Ancient Greek οἰκονομία from οἶκος (oikos, 'house') + νόμος (nomos, 'custom' or 'law'), hence 'rules of the house(hold)'. Current _____ models developed out of the broader field of political economy in the late 19th century, owing to a desire to use an empirical approach more akin to the physical sciences.
    a. Opportunity cost
    c. Energy economics
    b. Inflation
    d. Economic

12. _____ is the increase in the amount of the goods and services produced by an economy over time. It is conventionally measured as the percent rate of increase in real gross domestic product, or real GDP. Growth is usually calculated in real terms, i.e. inflation-adjusted terms, in order to net out the effect of inflation on the price of the goods and services produced.
    a. ACEA agreement
    c. ACCRA Cost of Living Index
    b. AD-IA Model
    d. Economic growth

13. _____ in its literal sense is the process of transformation of local or regional phenomena into global ones. It can be described as a process by which the people of the world are unified into a single society and function together.

This process is a combination of economic, technological, sociocultural and political forces.

    a. Global Cosmopolitanism
    c. Helsinki Process on Globalisation and Democracy
    b. Globally Integrated Enterprise
    d. Globalization

14. The term _____ is applied broadly to a variety of situations in which some financial institutions or assets suddenly lose a large part of their value. In the 19th and early 20th centuries, many financial crises were associated with banking panics, and many recessions coincided with these panics. Other situations that are often called financial crises include stock market crashes and the bursting of other financial bubbles, currency crises, and sovereign defaults.
    a. Co-operative economics
    c. Macroeconomics
    b. Market failure
    d. Financial crisis

15. A _____ is a geographical region that has economic laws that are more liberal than a country's typical economic laws. The category '_____' covers a broad range of more specific zone types, including Free Trade Zones (FTZ), Export Processing Zones (EPZ), Free Zones (FZ), Industrial Estates (IE), Free Ports, Urban Enterprise Zones and others. Usually the goal of a structure is to increase foreign investment.
    a. Special Economic Zone
    c. Transfer problem
    b. Linder hypothesis
    d. Customs union

Chapter 16. Making a Living in Developing Countries: Sustaining Growth, Enhancing Equity

16. The _____ is a trilateral trade bloc in North America created by the governments of the United States, Canada, and Mexico. The agreement creating the trade bloc came into force on January 1, 1994. It superseded the Canada-United States Free Trade Agreement between the U.S. and Canada.

 a. Case-Shiller Home Price Indices
 b. North American Free Trade Agreement
 c. Demand-side technologies
 d. Federal Reserve Bank Notes

17. _____ is the political interaction of transnational actors aimed at solving problems that affect more than one state or region when there is no power of enforcing compliance.

Traditionally, governance has been associated with 'governing,' or with political authority, institutions, and, ultimately, control. Governance in this particular sense denotes formal political institutions that aim to coordinate and control interdependent social relations and that have the ability to enforce decisions.

 a. Simultaneous policy
 b. Multilateralism
 c. 100-year flood
 d. Global governance

18. _____ relates to decisions that define expectations, grant power, or verify performance. It consists either of a separate process or of a specific part of management or leadership processes. Sometimes people set up a government to administer these processes and systems.

 a. 130-30 fund
 b. 100-year flood
 c. 1921 recession
 d. Governance

19. _____ is the concept or idea of fairness in economics, particularly as to taxation or welfare economics.

In welfare economics, _____ may be distinguished from economic efficiency in overall evaluation of social welfare. Although '_____' has broader uses, it may be posed as a counterpart to economic inequality in yielding a 'good' distribution of welfare.

 a. ACCRA Cost of Living Index
 b. ACEA agreement
 c. AD-IA Model
 d. Equity

20. In economics, _____ is how a natione;s total economy is distributed among its population. ._____ has always been a central concern of economic theory and economic policy. Classical economists such as Adam Smith, Thomas Malthus and David Ricardo were mainly concerned with factor _____, that is, the distribution of income between the main factors of production, land, labour and capital.

 a. Eco commerce
 b. Authorised capital
 c. Income distribution
 d. Equipment trust certificate

21. _____ is the body of laws, administrative rulings, and precedents which address the legal rights of, and restrictions on, working people and their organizations. As such, it mediates many aspects of the relationship between trade unions, employers and employees. In Canada, employment laws related to unionized workplaces are differentiated from those relating to particular individuals.

 a. Labour law
 b. 100-year flood
 c. 130-30 fund
 d. Labour movement

Chapter 16. Making a Living in Developing Countries: Sustaining Growth, Enhancing Equity

22. _____ is a forum for 21 Pacific Rim countries (styled 'member economies') to cooperate on regional trade and investment liberalisation and facilitation. APEC's objective is to enhance economic growth and prosperity in the region and to strengthen the Asia-Pacific community. Members account for approximately 40% of the world's population, approximately 54% of world GDP and about 44% of world trade.

   a. AD-IA Model
   b. ACEA agreement
   c. ACCRA Cost of Living Index
   d. Asia-Pacific Economic Cooperation

23. _____ is the transition to a more democratic political regime. It may be the transition from an authoritarian regime to a full democracy or transition from a semi-authoritarian political system to a democratic political system. The outcome may be consolidated or _____ may face frequent reversals (as it has faced for example in Argentina.)

   a. Democratization
   b. 130-30 fund
   c. 100-year flood
   d. 1921 recession

24. _____ is the a method of technical and economic research of the systems for purpose to optimize a parity between system's consumer functions or properties and expenses to achieve those functions or properties.

This methodology for continuous perfection of production, industrial technologies, organizational structures was developed by Juryj Sobolev in 1948 at the 'Perm telephone factory'

- 1948 Juryj Sobolev - the first success in application of a method analysis at the 'Perm telephone factory' .
- 1949 - the first application for the invention as result of use of the new method.

Today in economically developed countries practically each enterprise or the company use methodology of the kind of functional-cost analysis as a practice of the quality management, most full satisfying to principles of standards of series ISO 9000.

- Interest of consumer not in products itself, but the advantage which it will receive from its usage.
- The consumer aspires to reduce his expenses
- Functions needed by consumer can be executed in the various ways, and, hence, with various efficiency and expenses. Among possible alternatives of realization of functions exist such in which the parity of quality and the price is the optimal for the consumer.

The goal of _____ is achievement of the highest consumer satisfaction of production at simultaneous decrease in all kinds of industrial expenses Classical _____ has three English synonyms - Value Engineering, Value Management, Value Analysis.

   a. Function cost analysis
   b. Willingness to pay
   c. Staple financing
   d. Monopoly wage

25. _____ ndustrialization in North America, is the process of social and economic change whereby a human group is transformed from a pre-industrial society into an industrial one. _____ t is a part of a wider modernisation process, where social change and economic development are closely related with technological innovation, particularly with the development of large-scale energy and metallurgy production. _____ t is the extensive organisation of an economy for the purpose of manufacturing.

Chapter 16. Making a Living in Developing Countries: Sustaining Growth, Enhancing Equity

a. ACEA agreement
b. AD-IA Model
c. ACCRA Cost of Living Index
d. Industrialization

26. In economics, _____ refers to the ability of a person or a country to produce a particular good at a lower marginal cost and opportunity cost than another person or country. It is the ability to produce a product most efficiently given all the other products that could be produced. It can be contrasted with absolute advantage which refers to the ability of a person or a country to produce a particular good at a lower absolute cost than another.
   a. Triffin dilemma
   b. Comparative advantage
   c. Hot money
   d. Gravity model of trade

27. In international economics and international trade, _____ or _____ is the relative prices of a country's export to import. '_____' are sometimes used as a proxy for the relative social welfare of a country, but this heuristic is technically questionable and should be used with extreme caution. An improvement in a nation's _____ is good for that country in the sense that it has to pay less for the products it import.
   a. Common market
   b. Kennedy Round
   c. Terms of trade
   d. Commercial invoice

28. In microeconomics, _____ is quite simply the conversion of inputs into outputs. It is an economic process that uses resources to create a good or service that is suitable for exchange. This can include manufacturing, storing, shipping, and packaging.
   a. Solved
   b. Red Guards
   c. MET
   d. Production

29. _____ is a voluntary transfer of resources from one country to another, given at least partly with the objective of benefiting the recipient country. It may have other functions as well: it may be given as a signal of diplomatic approval, or to strengthen a military ally, to reward a government for behaviour desired by the donor, to extend the donor's cultural influence, to provide infrastructure needed by the donor for resource extraction from the recipient country, or to gain other kinds of commercial access. Humanitarianism and altruism are, nevertheless, significant motivations for the giving of _____.
   a. ACEA agreement
   b. AD-IA Model
   c. ACCRA Cost of Living Index
   d. Aid

30. _____ is that which is owed; usually referencing assets owed, but the term can also cover moral obligations and other interactions not requiring money. In the case of assets, _____ is a means of using future purchasing power in the present before a summation has been earned. Some companies and corporations use _____ as a part of their overall corporate finance strategy.
   a. Hard money loan
   b. Collateral Management
   c. Debt
   d. Debenture

31. The _____ consists of a number of economic theories which describe the nature of the firm, company including its existence, its behaviour, and its relationship with the market.

Chapter 16. Making a Living in Developing Countries: Sustaining Growth, Enhancing Equity 101

In simplified terms, the _____ aims to answer these questions:

1. Existence - why do firms emerge, why are not all transactions in the economy mediated over the market?
2. Boundaries - why the boundary between firms and the market is located exactly there? Which transactions are performed internally and which are negotiated on the market?
3. Organization - why are firms structured in such specific way? What is the interplay of formal and informal relationships?

Despite looking simple, these questions are not answered by the established economic theory, which usually views firms as given, and treats them as black boxes without any internal structure.

The First World War period saw a change of emphasis in economic theory away from industry-level analysis which mainly included analysing markets to analysis at the level of the firm, as it became increasingly clear that perfect competition was no longer an adequate model of how firms behaved. Economic theory till then had focussed on trying to understand markets alone and there had been little study on understanding why firms or organisations exist.

a. Theory of the firm
b. Policy Ineffectiveness Proposition
c. Technology gap
d. Khazzoom-Brookes postulate

32. A _____ is a duty imposed on goods when they are moved across a political boundary. They are usually associated with protectionism, the economic policy of restraining trade between nations. For political reasons, _____s are usually imposed on imported goods, although they may also be imposed on exported goods.
a. 130-30 fund
b. 100-year flood
c. 1921 recession
d. Tariff

Chapter 17. Making the World a Better Place

1. The _____ movement is movement of movements which are critical of the globalization of capitalism. Participants base their criticisms on a number of related ideas. What is shared is that participants stand in opposition to the unregulated political power of large, multi-national corporations and to the powers exercised through trade agreements.
   a. Overcapitalisation
   b. Asset price inflation
   c. Anti-globalization
   d. Anti-consumerism

2. _____ is that which is owed; usually referencing assets owed, but the term can also cover moral obligations and other interactions not requiring money. In the case of assets, _____ is a means of using future purchasing power in the present before a summation has been earned. Some companies and corporations use _____ as a part of their overall corporate finance strategy.
   a. Debt
   b. Debenture
   c. Collateral Management
   d. Hard money loan

3. _____s is the social science that studies the production, distribution, and consumption of goods and services. The term _____s comes from the Ancient Greek oá¼°κονομῐ́α from oá¼¶κος (oikos, 'house') + vῐ́Œμος (nomos, 'custom' or 'law'), hence 'rules of the house(hold)'. Current _____ models developed out of the broader field of political economy in the late 19th century, owing to a desire to use an empirical approach more akin to the physical sciences.
   a. Economic
   b. Energy economics
   c. Inflation
   d. Opportunity cost

4. The _____ is an international financial institution that provides financial and technical assistance to developing countries for development programs (e.g. bridges, roads, schools, etc.) with the stated goal of reducing poverty.

The _____ differs from the _____ Group, in that the _____ comprises only two institutions:

- International Bank for Reconstruction and Development (IBRD)
- International Development Association (IDA)

Whereas the latter incorporates these two in addition to three more:

- International Finance Corporation (IFC)
- Multilateral Investment Guarantee Agency (MIGA)
- International Centre for Settlement of Investment Disputes (ICSID)

John Maynard Keynes (right) represented the UK at the conference, and Harry Dexter White represented the US.

The _____ is one of two major financial institutions created as a result of the Bretton Woods Conference in 1944. The International Monetary Fund, a related but separate institution, is the second.

   a. Flow to Equity-Approach
   b. Bank-State-Branch
   c. Financial costs of the 2003 Iraq War
   d. World Bank

5. The _____ in Davos, Switzerland (January, 2003) triggered anti-globalization protests across Switzerland. Access to the town of Davos was blocked by the police of Grisons, with reinforcements from other cantons, and even Austrian police, which was unprecedented. On Saturday January 25, the day scheduled for a protest march in Davos, only selected protesters were allowed to pass.

a. 100-year flood
b. 130-30 fund
c. World Economic Forum
d. 1921 recession

6. The _____ is an important selective, mainly private, international organization designed by its founders to supervise and liberalize international trade. The organization officially commenced on 1 January 1995, under the Marrakesh Agreement, succeeding the 1947 General Agreement on Tariffs and Trade (GATT.)

The _____ deals with regulation of trade between participating countries; it provides a framework for negotiating and formalising trade agreements, and a dispute resolution process aimed at enforcing participants' adherence to _____ agreements which are signed by representatives of member governments and ratified by their parliaments.

a. Backus-Kehoe-Kydland consumption correlation puzzle
b. 2009 G-20 London summit protests
c. Bio-energy village
d. World Trade Organization

7. _____ is the political interaction of transnational actors aimed at solving problems that affect more than one state or region when there is no power of enforcing compliance.

Traditionally, governance has been associated with 'governing,' or with political authority, institutions, and, ultimately, control. Governance in this particular sense denotes formal political institutions that aim to coordinate and control interdependent social relations and that have the ability to enforce decisions.

a. Global governance
b. Simultaneous policy
c. 100-year flood
d. Multilateralism

8. _____ relates to decisions that define expectations, grant power, or verify performance. It consists either of a separate process or of a specific part of management or leadership processes. Sometimes people set up a government to administer these processes and systems.

a. 1921 recession
b. 130-30 fund
c. Governance
d. 100-year flood

9. _____ is a forum for 21 Pacific Rim countries (styled 'member economies') to cooperate on regional trade and investment liberalisation and facilitation. APEC's objective is to enhance economic growth and prosperity in the region and to strengthen the Asia-Pacific community. Members account for approximately 40% of the world's population, approximately 54% of world GDP and about 44% of world trade.

a. ACCRA Cost of Living Index
b. Asia-Pacific Economic Cooperation
c. AD-IA Model
d. ACEA agreement

10. _____ is the development of economic wealth of countries or regions for the well-being of their inhabitants. It is the process by which a nation improves the economic, political, and social well being of its people. From a policy perspective, _____ can be defined as efforts that seek to improve the economic well-being and quality of life for a community by creating and/or retaining jobs and supporting or growing incomes and the tax base.

a. Experimental economics
b. Economic methodology
c. Inflation
d. Economic Development

11. The _____ is an economic and political union of 27 member states, located primarily in Europe. It was established by the Treaty of Maastricht on 1 November 1993, upon the foundations of the pre-existing European Economic Community. With a population of almost 500 million, the _____ generates an estimated 30% share (US$18.4 trillion in 2008) of the nominal gross world product.

   a. ACEA agreement
   b. European Court of Justice
   c. ACCRA Cost of Living Index
   d. European Union

12. _____ is a type of trade policy that allows traders to act and transact without interference from government. Thus, the policy permits trading partners mutual gains from trade, with goods and services produced according to the theory of comparative advantage.

Under a _____ policy, prices are a reflection of true supply and demand, and are the sole determinant of resource allocation.

   a. 1921 recession
   b. 130-30 fund
   c. 100-year flood
   d. Free Trade

13. The _____ is a trilateral trade bloc in North America created by the governments of the United States, Canada, and Mexico. The agreement creating the trade bloc came into force on January 1, 1994. It superseded the Canada-United States Free Trade Agreement between the U.S. and Canada.

   a. Federal Reserve Bank Notes
   b. Case-Shiller Home Price Indices
   c. North American Free Trade Agreement
   d. Demand-side technologies

14. The _____ consists of a number of economic theories which describe the nature of the firm, company including its existence, its behaviour, and its relationship with the market.

In simplified terms, the _____ aims to answer these questions:

1. Existence - why do firms emerge, why are not all transactions in the economy mediated over the market?
2. Boundaries - why the boundary between firms and the market is located exactly there? Which transactions are performed internally and which are negotiated on the market?
3. Organization - why are firms structured in such specific way? What is the interplay of formal and informal relationships?

Despite looking simple, these questions are not answered by the established economic theory, which usually views firms as given, and treats them as black boxes without any internal structure.

The First World War period saw a change of emphasis in economic theory away from industry-level analysis which mainly included analysing markets to analysis at the level of the firm, as it became increasingly clear that perfect competition was no longer an adequate model of how firms behaved. Economic theory till then had focussed on trying to understand markets alone and there had been little study on understanding why firms or organisations exist.

a. Policy Ineffectiveness Proposition
b. Khazzoom-Brookes postulate
c. Technology gap
d. Theory of the firm

15. In finance, the _____ is the system that allows the transfer of money between savers and borrowers.

Put another way: the _____ is a set of complex and closely interconnected financial institutions, markets, instruments, services, practices, and transactions.

a. Financial system
b. Hedonimetry
c. Foreign investment
d. Lean consumption

16. _____ is the branch of economics that studies the dynamics of exchange rates, foreign investment, and how these affect international trade. It also studies international projects, international investments and capital flows, and trade deficits. It includes the study of futures, options and currency swaps.
a. Overshooting model
b. International finance
c. Optimum currency area
d. International investment position

17. The _____ is an international organization that oversees the global financial system by following the macroeconomic policies of its member countries, in particular those with an impact on exchange rates and the balance of payments. It is an organization formed to stabilize international exchange rates and facilitate development. It also offers financial and technical assistance to its members, making it an international lender of last resort.
a. ACCRA Cost of Living Index
b. ACEA agreement
c. Office of Thrift Supervision
d. International Monetary Fund

18. _____ is an economic system in which wealth, and the means of producing wealth, are privately owned. Through _____, the land, labor, and capital are owned, operated, and traded for the purpose of generating profits, without force or fraud, by private individuals either singly or jointly, and investments, distribution, income, production, pricing and supply of goods, commodities and services are determined by voluntary private decision in a market economy. A distinguishing feature of _____ is that each person owns his or her own labor and therefore is allowed to sell the use of it to employers.
a. Late capitalism
b. Socialism for the rich and capitalism for the poor
c. Creative capitalism
d. Capitalism

19. A _____, reserve bank, or monetary authority is the entity responsible for the monetary policy of a country or of a group of member states. It is a bank that can lend money to other banks in times of need. Its primary responsibility is to maintain the stability of the national currency and money supply, but more active duties include controlling subsidized-loan interest rates, and acting as a lender of last resort to the banking sector during times of financial crisis (private banks often being integral to the national financial system.)
a. 100-year flood
b. 1921 recession
c. Central bank
d. 130-30 fund

20. _____ is a concept in international development, political economy and international relations and describes the use of conditions attached to a loan, debt relief, bilateral aid or membership of international organizations, typically by the international financial institutions, regional organizations or donor countries.

_____ is typically employed by the International Monetary Fund, the World Bank or a donor country with respect to loans, debt relief and financial aid. Conditionalities may involve relatively uncontroversial requirements to enhance aid effectiveness, such as anti-corruption measures, but they may involve highly controversial ones, such as austerity or the privatization of key public services, which may provoke strong political opposition in the recipient country.

- a. Capacity Development
- b. Conditionality
- c. Sector-Wide Approach
- d. Participatory rural appraisal

21. In economics, an _____ is any good or commodity, transported from one country to another country in a legitimate fashion, typically for use in trade. _____ goods or services are provided to foreign consumers by domestic producers. _____ is an important part of international trade.
- a. ACCRA Cost of Living Index
- b. AD-IA Model
- c. ACEA agreement
- d. Export

22. A _____ is the transfer of wealth from one party (such as a person or company) to another. A _____ is usually made in exchange for the provision of goods, services or both, or to fulfill a legal obligation.

The simplest and oldest form of _____ is barter, the exchange of one good or service for another.

- a. Soft count
- b. Going concern
- c. Social gravity
- d. Payment

23. The _____ is an international organization of central banks which 'fosters international monetary and financial cooperation and serves as a bank for central banks.' It is not accountable to any national government. The BIS carries out its work through subcommittees, the secretariats it hosts, and through its annual General Meeting of all members. It also provides banking services, but only to central banks, or to international organizations like itself.
- a. Bank for International Settlements
- b. 100-year flood
- c. 1921 recession
- d. 130-30 fund

24. _____ is the practice within the banking industry of authorizing electronic transactions done with a debit card or credit card and holding this balance as unavailable either until the merchant clears the transaction _____s can fall off the account anywhere from 1-5 days after the transaction date depending on the bank's policy; in the case of credit cards, holds may last as long as 30 days, depending on the issuing bank.

Signature-based credit and debit card transactions are a two-step process, consisting of an authorization and a settlement.

When a merchant swipes a customer's credit card, the credit card terminal connects to the merchant's acquirer which verifies that the customer's account is valid and that sufficient funds are available to cover the transaction's cost.

- a. Electronic funds transfer
- b. Authorization hold
- c. Issuing bank
- d. Interbank network

Chapter 17. Making the World a Better Place

25. A _____ is the suggested tax on all trade of currency across borders. Named after the economist James Tobin, the tax is intended to put a penalty on short-term speculation in currencies. The original tax rate he proposed was 1%, which was subsequently lowered to between 0.1% and 0.25%.
    a. 130-30 fund
    b. 100-year flood
    c. Precarious work
    d. Tobin tax

26. The term _____ is applied broadly to a variety of situations in which some financial institutions or assets suddenly lose a large part of their value. In the 19th and early 20th centuries, many financial crises were associated with banking panics, and many recessions coincided with these panics. Other situations that are often called financial crises include stock market crashes and the bursting of other financial bubbles, currency crises, and sovereign defaults.
    a. Macroeconomics
    b. Financial crisis
    c. Co-operative economics
    d. Market failure

27. A _____ is an event or condition under the contract between a buyer and a seller to exchange an asset for payment. In accounting, it is recognized by an entry in the books of account. It involves a change in the status of the finances of two or more businesses or individuals.
    a. Present value of costs
    b. Financial transaction
    c. Negative gearing
    d. Biflation

28. To _____ is to impose a financial charge or other levy upon a taxpayer by a state or the functional equivalent of a state.

    _____es are also imposed by many subnational entities. _____es consist of direct _____ or indirect _____, and may be paid in money or as its labour equivalent (often but not always unpaid.)

    a. 1921 recession
    b. 100-year flood
    c. 130-30 fund
    d. Tax

29. _____ is a voluntary transfer of resources from one country to another, given at least partly with the objective of benefiting the recipient country. It may have other functions as well: it may be given as a signal of diplomatic approval, or to strengthen a military ally, to reward a government for behaviour desired by the donor, to extend the donor's cultural influence, to provide infrastructure needed by the donor for resource extraction from the recipient country, or to gain other kinds of commercial access. Humanitarianism and altruism are, nevertheless, significant motivations for the giving of _____.
    a. ACEA agreement
    b. Aid
    c. AD-IA Model
    d. ACCRA Cost of Living Index

30. The General Agreement on Tariffs and Trade was the outcome of the failure of negotiating governments to create the International Trade Organization (ITO.) _____ was formed in 1947 and lasted until 1994, when it was replaced by the World Trade Organization. The Bretton Woods Conference had introduced the idea for an organization to regulate trade as part of a larger plan for economic recovery after World War II.
    a. GATT
    b. General Agreement on Tariffs and Trade
    c. General Agreement on Trade in Services
    d. Dutch-Scandinavian Economic Pact

31. The _____ was the outcome of the failure of negotiating governments to create the International Trade Organization (ITO.) GATT was formed in 1947 and lasted until 1994, when it was replaced by the World Trade Organization. The Bretton Woods Conference had introduced the idea for an organization to regulate trade as part of a larger plan for economic recovery after World War II.
   a. Dutch-Scandinavian Economic Pact
   b. GATT
   c. General Agreement on Trade in Services
   d. General Agreement on Tariffs and Trade

32. A _____ is a geographical region that has economic laws that are more liberal than a country's typical economic laws. The category '_____' covers a broad range of more specific zone types, including Free Trade Zones (FTZ), Export Processing Zones (EPZ), Free Zones (FZ), Industrial Estates (IE), Free Ports, Urban Enterprise Zones and others. Usually the goal of a structure is to increase foreign investment.
   a. Linder hypothesis
   b. Transfer problem
   c. Customs union
   d. Special Economic Zone

33. A _____ is a duty imposed on goods when they are moved across a political boundary. They are usually associated with protectionism, the economic policy of restraining trade between nations. For political reasons, _____s are usually imposed on imported goods, although they may also be imposed on exported goods.
   a. 100-year flood
   b. 1921 recession
   c. 130-30 fund
   d. Tariff

34. In economics, _____ refers to the ability of a person or a country to produce a particular good at a lower marginal cost and opportunity cost than another person or country. It is the ability to produce a product most efficiently given all the other products that could be produced. It can be contrasted with absolute advantage which refers to the ability of a person or a country to produce a particular good at a lower absolute cost than another.
   a. Comparative advantage
   b. Triffin dilemma
   c. Hot money
   d. Gravity model of trade

35. _____ is the partial or total forgiveness of debt owed by individuals, corporations which started exploding with the Latin American debt crisis .

_____ for heavily indebted and underdeveloped developing countries was the subject in the 1990s of a campaign by a broad coalition of development NGOs, Christian organizations and others, under the banner of Jubilee 2000.

   a. Line of credit
   b. Debt consolidation
   c. Mexican Weekend
   d. Debt relief

36. _____ is exchange of capital, goods, and services across international borders or territories. In most countries, it represents a significant share of gross domestic product (GDP.) While _____ has been present throughout much of history , its economic, social, and political importance has been on the rise in recent centuries.
   a. Incoterms
   b. Intra-industry trade
   c. International trade
   d. Import license

37. The _____ is a treaty of the World Trade Organization (WTO) that entered into force in January 1995 as a result of the Uruguay Round negotiations. The treaty was created to extend the multilateral trading system to service sector, in the same way the General Agreement on Tariffs and Trade (GATT) provides such a system for merchandise trade.

All members of the WTO are signatories to the GATS.

a. General Agreement on Tariffs and Trade
b. Dutch-Scandinavian Economic Pact
c. GATT
d. General Agreement on Trade in Services

38. _____ are legal property rights over creations of the mind, both artistic and commercial, and the corresponding fields of law. Under _____ law, owners are granted certain exclusive rights to a variety of intangible assets, such as musical, literary, and artistic works; ideas, discoveries and inventions; and words, phrases, symbols, and designs. Common types of _____ include copyrights, trademarks, patents, industrial design rights and trade secrets.

a. Ease of Doing Business Index
b. Expedited Funds Availability Act
c. Intellectual Property
d. Independent contractor

39. A _____ is the exclusive authority to determine how a resource is used, whether that resource is owned by government or by individuals. All economic goods have a _____s attribute. This attribute has three broad components

1. The right to use the good
2. The right to earn income from the good
3. The right to transfer the good to others

The concept of _____s as used by economists and legal scholars are related but distinct. The distinction is largely seen in the economists' focus on the ability of an individual or collective to control the use of the good.

a. Property Right
b. High-reeve
c. Post-sale restraint
d. Holder in due course

40. The _____ commenced in September 1986 and continued until April 1994. The round, based on the General Agreement on Tariffs and Trade (GATT) ministerial meeting in Geneva (1982), was launched in Punta del Este in Uruguay (hence the name), followed by negotiations in Montreal, Geneva, Brussels, Washington, D.C., and Tokyo, with the 20 agreements finally being signed in Marrakech - the Marrakesh Agreement. The Round transformed the GATT into the World Trade Organization.

a. ACEA agreement
b. ACCRA Cost of Living Index
c. AD-IA Model
d. Uruguay Round

41. In microeconomics, _____ is quite simply the conversion of inputs into outputs. It is an economic process that uses resources to create a good or service that is suitable for exchange. This can include manufacturing, storing, shipping, and packaging.

a. Production
b. MET
c. Solved
d. Red Guards

110 Chapter 17. Making the World a Better Place

42. A _____ is:

- Rewrite _____, in generative grammar and computer science
- Standardization, a formal and widely-accepted statement, fact, definition, or qualification
- Operation, a determinate _____ for performing a mathematical operation and obtaining a certain result (Mathematics, Logic)
    - Unary operation
    - Binary operation
- _____ of inference, a function from sets of formulae to formulae (Mathematics, Logic)
- _____ of thumb, principle with broad application that is not intended to be strictly accurate or reliable for every situation. Also often simply referred to as a _____
- Moral, an atomic element of a moral code for guiding choices in human behavior
- Heuristic, a quantized '_____' which shows a tendency or probability for successful function
- A regulation, as in sports
- A Production _____, as in computer science
- Procedural law, a _____ set governing the application of laws to cases
    - A law, which may informally be called a '_____'
    - A court ruling, a decision by a court
- In the U.S. Government, a regulation mandated by Congress, but written or expanded upon by the Executive Branch.
- Norm (sociology), an informal but widely accepted _____, concept, truth, definition, or qualification (social norms, legal norms, coding norms)
- Norm (philosophy), a kind of sentence or a reason to act, feel or believe
- 'Rulership' is the concept of governance by a government:
    - Military _____, governance by a military body
    - Monastic _____, a collection of precepts that guides the life of monks or nuns in a religious order where the superior holds the place of Christ
- Slide _____

- '_____,' a song by Ayumi Hamasaki
- '_____,' a song by rapper Nas
- '_____s,' an album by the band The Whitest Boy Alive
- _____s: Pyaar Ka Superhit Formula, a 2003 Bollywood film
- ruler, an instrument for measuring lengths
- _____, a component of an astrolabe, circumferator or similar instrument
- The _____s, a bestselling self-help book
- _____ Project (Run Up-to-date Linux Everywhere), a project that aims to use up-to-date Linux software on old PCs
- _____ engine, a software system that helps managing business _____s
- Ja _____, a hip hop artist
    - R.U.L.E., a 2005 greatest hits album by rapper Ja _____
- '_____s,' a KMFDM song

a. Technocracy
b. Procter ' Gamble
c. Rule
d. Demand

43. A _____ is one scenario provided for evaluation by respondents in a Choice Experiment. Responses are collected and used to create a Choice Model. Respondents are usually provided with a series of differing _____s for evaluation.
   a. Choice Set
   b. 1921 recession
   c. 100-year flood
   d. 130-30 fund

44. The _____ was negotiated between members of the Organisation for Economic Co-operation and Development (OECD) between 1995 and 1998. Its purpose was to develop multilateral rules that would ensure international investment was governed in a more systematic and uniform way between states. When the first draft was leaked to the public in 1997, it drew widespread criticism from civil society groups and developing countries, particularly over the possibility that the agreement would make it difficult to regulate foreign investors.
   a. Trade barrier
   b. Multilateral Agreement on Investment
   c. Bilateral Investment Treaty
   d. Market access

45. _____ primarily refers to guidelines and interventions for the changing, maintenance or creation of living conditions that are conducive to human welfare. Thus, _____ is that part of public policy that has to do with social issues. The Malcolm Wiener Center for _____ at Harvard University describes it as 'public policy and practice in the areas of health care, human services, criminal justice, inequality, education, and labor' _____ is also distinct as an academic field.
   a. 1921 recession
   b. 100-year flood
   c. 130-30 fund
   d. Social Policy

46. _____ is any long-term change in the patterns of average weather of a specific region or the Earth as a whole. _____ reflects abnormal variations to the Earth's climate and subsequent effects on other parts of the Earth, such as in the ice caps over durations ranging from decades to millions of years.

In recent usage, especially in the context of environmental policy, _____ usually refers to changes in modern climate

   a. 130-30 fund
   b. 100-year flood
   c. 1921 recession
   d. Climate Change

47. The _____ is a protocol to the United Nations Framework Convention on Climate Change (UNFCCC or FCCC), an international environmental treaty produced at the United Nations Conference on treaty is intended to achieve 'stabilization of greenhouse gas concentrations in the atmosphere at a level that would prevent dangerous anthropogenic interference with the climate system.' The _____ establishes legally binding commitments for the reduction of four greenhouse gases (carbon dioxide, methane, nitrous oxide, sulphur hexafluoride), and two groups of gases (hydrofluorocarbons and perfluorocarbons) produced by 'Annex I' (industrialized) nations, as well as general commitments for all member countries. As of January 14 2009, 183 parties have ratified the protocol, which was initially adopted for use on 11 December 1997 in Kyoto, Japan and which entered into force on 16 February 2005. Under Kyoto, industrialized countries agreed to reduce their collective GHG emissions by 5.2% compared to the year 1990.
   a. Carbon offset
   b. Green New Deal
   c. Kyoto Protocol
   d. Greenhouse gases

Chapter 17. Making the World a Better Place

48. A _____ is a business that is privately owned and operated, with a small number of employees and relatively low volume of sales. The legal definition of 'small' often varies by country and industry, but is generally under 100 employees in the United States and under 50 employees in the European Union. In comparison, the definition of mid-sized business by the number of employees is generally under 500 in the U.S. and 250 for the European Union.
    a. Procurement
    b. Small Business
    c. Cabotage
    d. Farmshoring

49. _____ refer to the 'basic rights and freedoms to which all humans are entitled.' Examples of rights and freedoms which have come to be commonly thought of as _____ include civil and political rights, such as the right to life and liberty, freedom of expression, and equality before the law; and economic, social and cultural rights, including the right to participate in culture, the right to food, the right to work, and the right to education.

    The earliest sign of _____ has been found on the Cyrus Cylinder written during the reign of Cyrus the Great of Persia/Iran. The history of _____ dates back thousands of years and is judged based upon religious, cultural, philosophical and legal developments throughout the years.

    a. Commodity trading advisors
    b. Federal Reserve Bank Notes
    c. Dividend unit
    d. Human rights

50. The _____ is a specialized agency of the United Nations that deals with labour issues. Its headquarters are in Geneva, Switzerland. Its secretariat -- the people who are employed by it throughout the world -- is known as the International Labour Office.
    a. International Labour Organization
    b. ACEA agreement
    c. ACCRA Cost of Living Index
    d. AD-IA Model

51. _____ refers to the employment of children at regular and sustained labour. This practice is considered exploitative by many international organizations and is illegal in many countries. _____ was utilized to varying extents through most of history, but entered public dispute with the beginning of universal schooling, with changes in working conditions during industrialization, and with the emergence of the concepts of workers' and children's rights.
    a. Global march against child labor
    b. National Action Plan on the Elimination of Child Labour
    c. Debt bondage
    d. Child labour

52. _____ is a cross-disciplinary area concerned with protecting the safety, health and welfare of people engaged in work or employment. As a secondary effect, it may also protect co-workers, family members, employers, customers, suppliers, nearby communities, and other members of the public who are impacted by the workplace environment. It may involve interactions among many subject areas, including occupational medicine, occupational (or industrial) hygiene, public health, safety engineering, chemistry, health physics, ergonomics, toxicology, epidemiology, environmental health, industrial relations, public policy, sociology, and occupational health psychology.
    a. ACCRA Cost of Living Index
    b. ACEA agreement
    c. AD-IA Model
    d. Occupational safety and health

Chapter 17. Making the World a Better Place

53. _____ ndustrialization in North America, is the process of social and economic change whereby a human group is transformed from a pre-industrial society into an industrial one. _____ t is a part of a wider modernisation process, where social change and economic development are closely related with technological innovation, particularly with the development of large-scale energy and metallurgy production. _____ t is the extensive organisation of an economy for the purpose of manufacturing.
   a. AD-IA Model
   b. Industrialization
   c. ACEA agreement
   d. ACCRA Cost of Living Index

54. _____ is the increase in the average temperature of the Earth's near-surface air and oceans since the mid-twentieth century and its projected continuation. Global surface temperature increased 0.74 ± 0.18 °C (1.33 ± 0.32 °F) during the last century. The Intergovernmental Panel on Climate Change (IPCC) concludes that anthropogenic greenhouse gases are responsible for most of the observed temperature increase since the middle of the twentieth century, and that natural phenomena such as solar variation and volcanoes probably had a small warming effect from pre-industrial times to 1950 and a small cooling effect afterward.
   a. Controlled Foreign Corporations
   b. Dividend unit
   c. Consumer goods
   d. Global warming

55. _____ is the increase in the amount of the goods and services produced by an economy over time. It is conventionally measured as the percent rate of increase in real gross domestic product, or real GDP. Growth is usually calculated in real terms, i.e. inflation-adjusted terms, in order to net out the effect of inflation on the price of the goods and services produced.
   a. ACCRA Cost of Living Index
   b. AD-IA Model
   c. Economic growth
   d. ACEA agreement

56. _____ is the concept or idea of fairness in economics, particularly as to taxation or welfare economics.

In welfare economics, _____ may be distinguished from economic efficiency in overall evaluation of social welfare. Although '_____' has broader uses, it may be posed as a counterpart to economic inequality in yielding a 'good' distribution of welfare.

   a. ACCRA Cost of Living Index
   b. Equity
   c. ACEA agreement
   d. AD-IA Model

57. _____ in its literal sense is the process of transformation of local or regional phenomena into global ones. It can be described as a process by which the people of the world are unified into a single society and function together.

This process is a combination of economic, technological, sociocultural and political forces.

   a. Globally Integrated Enterprise
   b. Global Cosmopolitanism
   c. Helsinki Process on Globalisation and Democracy
   d. Globalization

ANSWER KEY

Chapter 1
1. d   2. d   3. d   4. a   5. b   6. b   7. c   8. a   9. d   10. d
11. a 12. a 13. c 14. d 15. d 16. d 17. d 18. d 19. b 20. d
21. b 22. d 23. d

Chapter 2
1. c   2. d   3. d   4. d   5. d   6. d   7. d   8. a   9. d   10. a
11. d 12. b 13. d 14. d 15. a 16. b 17. a 18. a 19. a 20. d
21. d 22. b 23. b 24. c 25. d 26. c 27. d 28. d

Chapter 3
1. d   2. b   3. d   4. d   5. d   6. d   7. d   8. d   9. d   10. a
11. a 12. d 13. b 14. a 15. a 16. c 17. a 18. d 19. d 20. d
21. d

Chapter 4
1. d   2. d   3. d   4. a   5. d   6. d   7. a   8. d   9. d   10. b
11. c 12. d 13. d 14. d 15. a 16. b 17. d 18. b 19. b 20. d
21. d 22. d 23. c 24. d 25. a 26. a 27. a 28. a 29. b 30. a
31. d 32. b 33. b 34. a 35. d 36. d 37. c 38. d 39. d 40. d
41. b 42. b 43. d 44. b 45. d 46. d 47. d 48. a 49. a 50. b
51. d 52. a 53. d

Chapter 5
1. c   2. d   3. c   4. c   5. a   6. d   7. a   8. b   9. a   10. d
11. b 12. d 13. b 14. d 15. b 16. d 17. a 18. d 19. c 20. d
21. c 22. b 23. d 24. d 25. d 26. a 27. c 28. d 29. c 30. d
31. c 32. d 33. b 34. d 35. d 36. a 37. d 38. d 39. d 40. d
41. a 42. d 43. d 44. d 45. a 46. d 47. a 48. c 49. c 50. a
51. b 52. b 53. b 54. b 55. d 56. d

Chapter 6
1. d   2. b   3. c   4. d   5. d   6. d   7. a   8. d   9. d   10. b
11. d 12. d 13. b 14. b 15. b 16. a 17. c 18. a 19. b 20. a
21. a 22. d 23. c 24. b 25. c 26. b 27. d 28. d 29. d 30. a
31. d 32. d 33. b 34. d 35. d

Chapter 7
1. d   2. a   3. c   4. d   5. a   6. a   7. d   8. d   9. a   10. d
11. c 12. d 13. d 14. d 15. d 16. d 17. a 18. a 19. b 20. d
21. d 22. d 23. a 24. a

Chapter 8
1. d   2. b   3. c   4. d   5. b   6. d   7. c   8. b   9. d   10. c
11. a 12. d 13. d 14. a 15. d 16. d 17. d 18. d 19. a 20. a
21. d 22. b 23. b 24. c 25. c 26. c 27. d 28. d 29. c

ANSWER KEY

Chapter 9
1. d   2. c   3. a   4. c   5. d   6. d   7. c   8. d   9. d   10. d
11. b   12. c   13. c   14. d   15. d   16. d   17. b   18. c   19. a   20. d
21. d   22. d   23. a   24. d   25. c   26. d   27. d   28. d   29. b

Chapter 10
1. b   2. d   3. d   4. a   5. d   6. a   7. c   8. b   9. c   10. c
11. c   12. b   13. a   14. d   15. d   16. d   17. d   18. a   19. c   20. d
21. d   22. d   23. b   24. d   25. a

Chapter 11
1. b   2. d   3. a   4. b   5. b   6. a   7. a   8. d   9. c   10. d
11. a   12. a   13. b   14. d   15. d   16. d   17. a   18. b   19. d   20. c

Chapter 12
1. d   2. b   3. d   4. b   5. c   6. a   7. d   8. b   9. a   10. d
11. d   12. a   13. c   14. b   15. d   16. a   17. b   18. d   19. d   20. b
21. d   22. c   23. b   24. c   25. c   26. b   27. d   28. a   29. c   30. a
31. a   32. a   33. c   34. d   35. a   36. d   37. c   38. c   39. d   40. d
41. c

Chapter 13
1. d   2. d   3. d   4. c   5. d   6. b   7. d   8. b   9. d   10. d
11. a   12. d   13. d   14. d   15. d   16. c   17. d   18. c   19. d   20. d
21. a   22. d   23. a   24. d   25. a

Chapter 14
1. d   2. a   3. d   4. d   5. d   6. d   7. d   8. a   9. a   10. a
11. d   12. d   13. d

Chapter 15
1. b   2. a   3. d   4. d   5. b   6. d   7. c   8. d   9. a   10. d
11. d   12. a   13. d   14. d   15. d   16. d   17. b   18. c   19. a   20. d
21. b   22. a   23. d   24. a   25. b

Chapter 16
1. c   2. d   3. d   4. a   5. a   6. a   7. a   8. d   9. b   10. c
11. d   12. d   13. d   14. d   15. a   16. b   17. d   18. d   19. d   20. c
21. a   22. d   23. a   24. a   25. d   26. b   27. c   28. d   29. d   30. c
31. a   32. d

Chapter 17

1. c	2. a	3. a	4. d	5. c	6. d	7. a	8. c	9. b	10. d
11. d	12. d	13. c	14. d	15. a	16. b	17. d	18. d	19. c	20. b
21. d	22. d	23. a	24. b	25. d	26. b	27. b	28. d	29. b	30. a
31. d	32. d	33. d	34. a	35. d	36. c	37. d	38. c	39. a	40. d
41. a	42. c	43. a	44. b	45. d	46. d	47. c	48. b	49. d	50. a
51. d	52. d	53. b	54. d	55. c	56. b	57. d			

www.ingramcontent.com/pod-product-compliance
Lightning Source LLC
Chambersburg PA
CBHW082127230426

43671CB00015B/2825